What People are saying about

Isis

The Egyptian goddess Ma'at [...] Truth and Balance but her name also re[...]ng balance in the universe (as opposed to chaos). [...] my mind this book serves Ma'at as much as Isis, aiming for a welcome balance between scholarly sources and contemporary Pagan perspectives. It informs the readers that the original Egyptian name of Isis was Aset but also provides suggestions for performing contemporary rituals dedicated to Isis. Isis is both ancient and timeless. Olivia Church writes with the mind of a scholar and the heart of a devotee!

Imelda Almqvist, international teacher and author of *Natural Born Shamans: A Spiritual Toolkit for Life* and *Sacred Art: A Hollow Bone for Spirit*

Olivia's knowledge on ancient Egypt and its mythology comes in second only to her passion for the subject, which the reader can almost taste as they digest her words. Intellectual, educational and exquisitely presented.

Mandi See, author of *Eclectic Wicca, A Guide for the Modern Witch*

Olivia Church's outstanding book is the perfect introduction to the history and worship of Isis. Church writes authoritatively about the goddess, giving readers a thorough yet accessible grounding in Egyptian documentation and archaeology before exploring how Isis changed over time. The academic content of the work is presented with rigour and clarity, showing Church's deep understanding of her topic. Each chapter finishes with the content being refocused through a contemporary Pagan perspective, making the work come alive in our modern spiritual context. The final section, where Church explores how Isis could

be worshipped today, gives the piece a very practical feel and encourages the reader to explore Isis through their own practice.
Andrew Anderson, author of *The Ritual of Writing*

Pagan Portals
Isis

Great of Magic, She of 10,000 Names

Pagan Portals
Isis

Great of Magic, She of 10,000 Names

Olivia Church

MOON
BOOKS

Winchester, UK
Washington, USA

JOHN HUNT PUBLISHING

First published by Moon Books, 2021
Moon Books is an imprint of John Hunt Publishing Ltd., No. 3 East Street, Alresford
Hampshire SO24 9EE, UK
office@jhpbooks.net
www.johnhuntpublishing.com
www.moon-books.net

For distributor details and how to order please visit the 'Ordering' section on our website.

A CIP catalogue record for this book is available from the British Library.

Design: Stuart Davies

UK: Printed and bound by CPI Group (UK) Ltd, Croydon, CR0 4YY
Printed in North America by CPI GPS partners

We operate a distinctive and ethical publishing philosophy in
all areas of our business, from our global network of authors to
production and worldwide distribution.

Contents

This book is dedicated to my dear friend Ronnie, a wise woman, a source of inspiration, and the compass which always leads me back to Egypt.

Foreword and Acknowledgements

As a child I was in awe of the ancient Egyptians and anything to do with the ancient world. This blossomed into love during my adolescence where I discovered that the stories and beliefs of the ancients spoke to me far more than those of the Anglican Church that I grew up with (although my family were not particularly religious). As I discovered Paganism it seemed natural for me to begin my journey with the Egyptian Gods and Goddesses I had loved learning about, with Isis being first among them. It is this personal piety that prompted me to ask more questions about Egyptian religion and the ancient Egyptians themselves. I went on to study this at University for my Bachelor's and Master's degrees. My doctoral research into contemporary Pagan (or 'neo-Pagan') interactions with archaeology is a development from this passion. With this background, my approach to ancient Egypt is two-fold, from a modern Pagan perspective, to a scholarly Egyptological one. I always endeavour to keep the distinction between the two clear. When writing about personal gnosis or contemporary Pagan ideas relating to Egypt I specify as such.

As a part of the Pagan Portals series, I aim for this book to be accessible for Pagan readers called to worship Isis, as well as those generally interested in her ancient and modern worship. I will approach this by combining and distinguishing between scholarly sources and contemporary Pagan perspectives. In this way, I hope that you as the reader can appreciate both ancient and modern views of how Isis manifests in the world.

I owe my thanks to Jenny, who recommended me for this work, and to the Egyptology staff in Swansea University, and the Egypt Centre, who taught me to read hieroglyphs and made ancient Egypt tangible. I thank my dear friend Ronnie, who has encouraged me in my studies of the Goddesses and Gods of Egypt, both with academic tenacity and spiritual ardour. And

I thank my mam, who bought my first published poem and has believed in my writing throughout my life.

Ankh, Wuja, Seneb
Life, Prosperity, Health

Abbreviations

PT – Pyramid Texts
CT – Coffin Texts
BD – Book of the Dead
PCB – Papyrus Chester Beatty
BRP – Bremner-Rhind Papyrus
Met – Metamorphoses (by Apuleius)

Timeline

Dates provided from Shaw, 2003:

Early Dynasty Period
Comprising Dynasties 1 & 2, 3000-2686 BCE

Old Kingdom
Comprising Dynasties 3-8, 2686-2160 BCE

First Intermediate Period
Comprising Dynasties 9 & 10, 2160-2055 BCE

Middle Kingdom
Comprising Dynasties 11-14, 2055-1650 BCE

Second Intermediate Period
Comprising Dynasties 15-17, 1650-1550 BCE

New Kingdom – (Including Ramesside Period)
Comprising Dynasties 18-20, 1550-1069 BCE

Third Intermediate Period
Comprising Dynasties 21-25, 1069-664 BCE

Late Period
Comprising Dynasties 26-30 & 2nd Persian Period, 664-332 BCE

Graeco-Roman Period
Comprising Macedonian & Ptolemaic Dynasties, 332-30 BCE;
Roman Period, 30 BCE – 395 CE

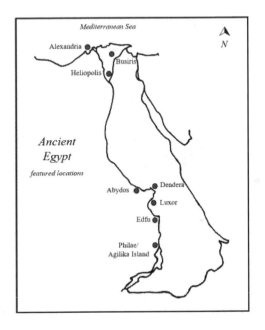

Map of Featured Ancient Egyptian Sites

Introduction

Setting the Scene

The name 'Isis' is one that is recognised by most people in the Western world. Without much effort, many can conjure up ideas associated with this name, whether it be images of a golden winged Goddess, the story of a God's murder, or descriptions of ancient Egyptian temples. This is partly down to her popularity in the ancient Mediterranean, which has had an enduring influence on Western cultures to this day. Another explanation for her survival is that she is incredibly relatable and approachable to all kinds of people, from the past and the present. There is a reason why her cult extended far beyond Egypt and was still remembered during the Middle Ages, when other Pagan cults had been lost to antiquity (Clauss, 2000).

The image we have of Isis is one which has been coloured heavily by ancient Graeco-Roman perceptions. The Goddess known as Aset, wove her magic through Egyptian culture for millennia, before the Greeks and Romans adopted her into their own religious systems, reinterpreting and re-naming her "Isis". This Graeco-Roman form is the common image that we have inherited of Aset today, in part because this period of time (332 BCE – 395 CE) was when her cults were at their most widespread both within and beyond Egypt. On the other hand, however, such reinterpretations have perpetuated a Mediterranean portrait of Aset, following the antiquarian trend of claiming Egyptian heritage for Eurocentric narratives of history. It is therefore essential that we collectively reclaim Aset's North African Egyptian origins, understanding that her development into Isis is a testament of North African influences on ancient Mediterranean religions, and giving credit to this cultural heritage.

The name 'Isis' itself is of Graeco-Roman origin. Her original Egyptian name was Aset. The Egyptian form of Aset was quite different from her latter manifestations, though she always retained her core essence. This Goddess went through a considerable transformation and shapeshifted to such an extent that she became known as Isis of 10,000 names, identified with countless other Goddesses. In Apuleius' *'Metamorphoses'*, (abbreviated hereafter, *Met*) better known as, *'The Golden Ass'*, Isis expresses this herself:

"I, the mother of the universe, mistress of all the elements, and first offspring of the ages; mightiest of deities, queen of the dead, and foremost of heavenly beings; my one person manifests the aspect of all gods and goddesses." (Apuleius, *Met* 11:5-6)

If Isis is a shapeshifting universal Goddess, what makes Her unique, what powers does she possess, and what is Isis a Goddess of? Firstly, Isis is a Goddess of magic *par excellence*. Her magic weaves its way through each of her stories, through acts of trickery, healing, regeneration, and transformation. She is also a Goddess of grief, of divine love, motherhood, protection, and sovereignty. Isis flies between life and death, and warring gods. Her empathy reaches royal families, priests, and common people, who are all united in their shared human experiences: of love gained and lost, families built and torn apart, the quest for knowledge, and the dignity of personal autonomy.

The Ancient Egyptian Context

Despite overlaying Mediterranean concepts upon Isis' character and iconography, she never lost touch with her Egyptian roots. Isis and her cult remained exotic and foreign outside of Egypt, perhaps adding to her appeal as well as her condemnation.

Ancient Egyptian ideology and religious ideas were born from how the occupants of the Nile Valley interpreted the natural and societal world around them. Isis' origins are firmly planted in the soil and sands of the Egyptian landscape. The context of her homeland is important to understand if one is to appreciate her genesis fully. Located in the northeast corner of Africa, Egypt was surrounded by influencing cultures, such as the people of Sudan to the south, Libya in the west, the Mediterranean in the north and the multitude of near eastern cultures to the east. The Nile River with its rich flood plain lies at the heart of Egypt, which is otherwise surrounded by arid desert. As a result of Neolithic climate change, Egypt's savannah landscape dried out, leading communities of people closer to the Nile as the primary source of life (Craig Patch, 2011).

Egypt's ancient river cuts through the centre of the valley, flowing from the south (Upper Egypt) to the north (Lower Egypt). The river expands out into a flood plain, cradled on either side by sandy hills; beyond these lie the Saharan desert to the west, and ancient wadis leading east to the Red Sea. The sun would rise over the top of the eastern mountains, peaking above the Nile, and setting behind the mountains in the west; this created an image of the sun rising and setting from within the earth itself. In the months of August through to December, the season of *Akhet*, the Nile would flood, covering the agricultural lands in water. The water brought dark silt to the floodplain, re-fertilising the land. This was the inspiration for the Egyptians' calling their country *Kemet*, the black land (Craig Patch, 2011). Once the water receded from January to April, the Egyptians planted new crops, during a season aptly named, *Peret*, 'emerging' or 'coming forth'. Finally came the season of *Shomu*, where these crops would be harvested (Brewer & Teeter, 2007).

The Egyptian summer would have then been too hot and dry for life to thrive and so the next flood was highly anticipated for agricultural renewal. This perpetual cycle taught the Egyptians that as the plants grew, died, and grew again, so too would they live, die, and live again. The hot summer brought endings, dried fields, and diseases, whilst the cool winter heralded growth, water, and prosperity.

In addition to understanding Egypt's landscape, one should be aware that ancient Egyptian history spans from around 3000 BCE to 30 CE. We oftentimes like to maintain an unchanging romanticised image of ancient Egypt; however, 3000 years is an incredible amount of time for a human society. The people of Cleopatra VII's Egypt would be further away in time from the people of the Old Kingdom, than we are today from the ancient Romans! Naturally the cult of Isis would have gone through considerable changes from her first attestation in the Old Kingdom, to her influence in the Roman world.

* * *

In this book I will predominantly refer to the Goddess in question under the name of Isis, rather than the original Egyptian, Aset. This is in to be consistent with the book's title, which I hope will attract readers interested in Aset-Isis's historical journey, and in doing so, present the opportunity to teach readers about her distinctively Egyptian origins, as well as her later Graeco-Roman developments. Her mythology and cult will be introduced, as well as festivals and rituals that may be relevant to her followers today. I hope that within these pages Isis speaks to you as an intrigued reader and inspires you to reflect on why this 4500-year-old Goddess, continues to be relevant to people across the globe today.

Chapter 1

Mythology: Creation & Great of Magic

To fully understand the character of Isis one must read her mythology to see how she interacts with other deities and how she faces the many challenges that are thrown her way. Her story must begin with creation, setting the scene for how her divine family came to be. Following on from her birth, it doesn't take Isis long to build a reputation as one of great cleverness. How she came to be known as Isis, Great of Magic, is essential to her whole being, and to every chapter of her mythology thereafter.

The Sources of Isis & Osiris' Mythology

The key chapters of Isis and Osiris' story are scattered throughout multiple Egyptian and Greek sources. The most complete telling of the story from native Egyptian literature is from a New Kingdom hymn (1550-1225 BCE) from the stela of an elite man named, Amenmose (Lichtheim, 1976). Much later, Greek historians such as Diodorus Siculus and Plutarch expand upon this narrative in more detail, inevitably adding their own Greek flare to the stories (Swetnam-Burland, 2015). It is therefore to be expected that the story changed through the centuries and the different authors retelling it. Today we hear the myth through our own culture's filters of understanding, adding depth and relevance to the story for each person who hears it. The myth of Isis and Osiris is a famous one, for good reason.

The Heliopolitan Creation Myth

Heliopolis was a town known as *Iunu* to the ancient Egyptians and was located to the northwest of modern-day Cairo (Wilkinson, 2000). This was the cult centre for the Heliopolitan Ennead, a group of nine deities whose mythology forms the backdrop of the Isis-Osiris story. Recorded as early as the Old Kingdom *Pyramid Texts* (abbreviated hereafter, *PT*) is the myth of how the God Atum-Ra formed new life from a self-creative act, either through masturbation or spitting (*PT* 527 and 600). This resulted in the birth of his two children, Shu and Tefnut, the divine personifications of air and moisture. The pair wandered away from their father, causing him such distress that he sent his Eye (the embodied sun disk, named the Eye of Ra) to go in search of them. Upon their return, the Eye discovered that her father had replaced her with another; to placate her anger at this betrayal, Atum-Ra placed her upon his head as the first Uraeus serpent (Pinch, 2002).

Following on from this interlude, Shu and Tefnut came together and from their union sprung another pairing, Nut the Sky Goddess and Geb the earth God. This is an interesting example of how the Egyptians thought in a different way to cultures such as the Greeks and Romans, who traditionally viewed the earth as feminine and sky as masculine (Barthell, 1971). In early afterlife ideology the king was believed to be reborn by the sky Goddess Nut and ascended to join the imperishable stars of her body (Pinch, 2002). This may be why the sky was considered a mother, instead of the earth.

Nut and Geb held one another in such a close embrace that no life could exist between them. Their father, Shu decided to intervene, lifting Nut's body high above the earth. This great cosmological event is illustrated repeatedly in Egyptian religious art. Once the two were separated, Nut could finally give birth to the offspring that they had conceived. In a later development of the *PT* known as the *Coffin Texts*, (abbreviated hereafter, *CT* and dated to the Middle Kingdom) Nut had been forbidden by Ra to give birth on any day of the 360-day year. Fortunately, the wise God Thoth came to her aid. Through a board game with the moon God, Thoth was able to win Nut five more days of the year to give birth to her offspring, bringing the year up to total 365 days (Pinch, 2002).

It is on these five epagomenal days that Isis and her siblings were brought into existence. First born was Osiris who would inherit the throne of the earth from his father Geb; second came Horus the Elder (later named the uncle of Horus son of Isis); third came Set, who burst forth violently from his mother (Plutarch, *Isis and Osiris* 12); fourth was Isis and finally Nephthys came on the fifth and final day (Pinch, 2002). Thus, were the Heliopolitan Ennead brought forth into creation and the stories of Isis began to unravel.

Isis learns Ra's Secret Name

The non-linear style of Egyptian mythology presents a period where the Ennead co-existed during Ra's reign on earth. Shu had not yet taken the throne, nor had his son Geb or grandson Osiris. Despite being the supreme God and possessing great creative magic, Ra had three generations of deities beneath him and his age had begun to show. Isis was already renowned for knowing everything "in the sky and on the earth" (*CT* 411; Faulkner, 2007); that is, everything except the true, secret name of Ra.

A key religious concept throughout ancient Egyptian history is the belief in the power of the spoken and written word. Words had the power to manifest into reality, and someone's name, their *ren*, was as much a living part of them as their physical, or spiritual bodies (Ikram, 2003). To know and speak the Creator's true name was to possess a considerable piece of his great magic and to have power over him. For this reason, Ra kept his name a close secret so that none would have access to such power:

"I hid it in my body when I was born to prevent the power of any male or female magician coming to be against me."
(Ritner, 2008, p. 22)

Isis was always seeking to learn more and desired to become

a great magician. Naturally, her attention turned to this tantalising piece of hidden information and all that it promised in its discovery. The *Turin Magical Papyrus*, dating to the New Kingdom, records a spell to protect the user against poisonous creatures (Pinch, 2006). Within this spell, the myth of how Isis gained knowledge of Ra's true name is revealed. Being the creator of all things, Ra was invulnerable to the venoms of every one of his creations; in other words, none could do him harm, but himself. Unfortunately for Ra, Isis was aware of this. Ra had begun to dribble in his old age, which Isis had also noticed. The clever Goddess concocted an ingenious plan that would force Ra to reveal his true name to her. Whilst he was sleeping, Isis caught some of his spittle and magically fashioned a serpent from it. The next day she covertly placed the serpent at his feet, whereupon it bit him with his own poison, the only thing with the power to harm or kill him. Feigning innocence, the Goddess came to his aid insisting that the only way she could heal him was if she knew the true name of the thing that was killing him. Ra offered up several epithets, desperately avoiding betraying his own secret. It was no use. Finally, in desperation he conceded to reveal his true name to Isis, under the proviso that she would pass this on to none, save for her future son and the heir of Egypt's throne (Pinch, 2002).

Whilst Isis hears the secret name whispered into her ear, we human readers are left in the dark, for the Egyptian texts omit recording the Creator's true name. The fact that Isis is in possession of this name is of great significance. In knowing the name of everything in existence, Isis herself becomes a Creatrix, with power over all things. As a result of her ingenious trickery through magical means, Isis thereafter earns the title 'Great of Magic,' *Weret-Hekau*. Gifted with the knowledge of Ra's secret name, the Goddess's speech is ever empowered by *heka*, a concept we could loosely translate as 'magic'. By her word alone she performs great protective spells:

"His sister [Isis] was his guard, She who drives off the foes, Who stops the deeds of the disturbed By the power of her utterance. The clever-tongued whose speech fails not..."
(*Papyrus Ebers* 2; trans. Lichtheim, 1976, pp. 85)

As seen above, if Isis can save the Creator from harm, she must have the power to spare her devotees from danger also. From this moment on, Isis repulses the threat of poisons through the power of her speech:

"Every reptile with stings listens to me... Isis, great of magic before the gods, has spoken, to whom Geb has given his magic to repulse poison. Be powerless, be repulsed, retreat, flee back, poison!"
(*Metternich Stela* 210-211; Scott, p. 211)

These magical abilities become essential as her mythological narrative continues.

Magic & Heka

Before Isis' story further unfolds, it is important to address the concept of *heka*, which Isis is 'Great of'. *Heka* is often translated simply as 'magic', but definitions of magic are not so simple at all. What really is magic? To the Egyptians, *heka* was recognised as a force which, like many other concepts, could be personified as a deity (Pinch, 2006). *Heka* is a force, a palpable energy which the Creator formed in order to help his creations through life's trials:

"He made for them magic as weapons To ward off the blow of events, Guarding them by day and by night."
(*The Instruction Addressed to King Merikare*; Lichtheim, 1973, p. 106)

In this regard magic can be understood as a natural force to be harnessed in order to cause change in one's life. It is not inherently good or bad. There is no black or white *heka*. *Heka* is a neutral force and it is the action which is done through using it that can be judged against one's subjective morality. Spell 125 of the *Book of the Dead* (abbreviated hereafter, *BD*) contains a text known as the *Negative Confession* and provides us with clues to what the Egyptians of the time deemed morally reprehensible (Kelly Simpson, et al. 2003). Generally speaking, upholding the balance of *ma'at* was the most important thing of all. The concept of *ma'at* was personified by the Goddess Ma'at, Goddess of truth and balance. Maintaining *ma'at* meant ensuring the balance of the universe was kept, both in light and in dark, in life and in death. Despite her cunning ways, as a great granddaughter of the Sun God, Isis would use the power of *heka* within the balance of *ma'at,* manipulating her magic for the good of all.

Isis' magical skills were intrinsically woven into each of her myths and whether she was fulfilling the role of queen, mother, saviour, or a funerary Goddess, she was always the magician. As a queen and defender of the natural order of things she was filled with sovereign *heka*; as a funerary Goddess she had the power to breathe life back into the dead; as a mother she used *heka* to heal and protect her son during his many trials. To the ancient Egyptians Isis was a magician, trained in her craft. Not only was she imbued with intrinsic divine power, she also *practiced* and *learnt* her magical craft, through mastering the correct rituals, and obtaining secret knowledge from the Creator. For this reason, Isis was believed to be "more powerful than a thousand soldiers" (Pinch, 2006, p. 29) and truly *Great of Magic*.

Isis & Osiris Rule Egypt

The story now leaves the themes of creation and enters the time when Nut and Geb's first born son Osiris, ascends to the throne of earth. Each of their offspring were paired off together, as with most Egyptian deities. The Egyptians believed that duality maintained the balance of life, of *ma'at*, and so most deities were placed in opposite-sex pairings. It is worth noting that the emphasis is less on heterosexual coupling and more on the balance of perceived opposites in an Egyptian worldview. In the case of the Ennead, Osiris and Isis are said to have fallen in love in the womb (Plutarch, *Isis and Osiris* 12); contrastingly, Set and Nephthys appear to have been paired with little affection. In some versions Horus the Elder is omitted and Horus the Younger completes the Ennead as the son of Osiris (Pinch, 2006). When he *is* included, Horus the Elder is the remaining fifth member and so is paired outside of the Ennead with Ra's daughter, Hathor. This may be because he is a God pre-dating the Heliopolitan Ennead structure. The Egyptians had no problem with multiple versions of myths and Gods, especially as they would have varied according to time and place anyway.

Although Isis' motherhood of Horus appears from her origins in the Old Kingdom 5th Dynasty (2495-2345 BCE), it wasn't until the following Dynasty that her marriage to Osiris became canon (Lesko, 1999). Today the couple are often pictured as the ultimate *hieros gamos*, the Divine Couple who complete one another in sexual duality and partnership. Sadly, lover's bliss is relatively short-lived for these two and their story is not one that I personally would want to identify my own relationships with, as will be clear in the next chapter.

Isis and Osiris mythologically reigned together as benevolent rulers who taught the invaluable secrets of agriculture to the Egyptians (McCabe, 2008). Their rule encompassed the entire fertile stretch of the Nile Valley, in the area considered *within* the order of creation. Anything beyond this was regarded as foreign, potentially dangerous, and a place of chaos. This was the realm given to their brother, Set. Set was envious of his elder brother's throne and fertile land. This jealousy is something which Plutarch emphasised by recording an additional subplot to the story, telling of how Set's consort Nephthys cuckolded him with Osiris. Plutarch claims that Nephthys was in love with Osiris and disguised herself as her twin sister in order to lay beside him at night. From this secret union the jackal-headed God Anubis was said to have been conceived. Isis discovered this but chose to act from a place of compassion. Wanting to avoid Set's wrath and not desiring to abandon the child, the two sisters raised Anubis together (Plutarch, *Isis and Osiris* 14). This God would prove useful later in the narrative, as he became patron of embalmers...

A Contemporary Pagan Perspective

There are numerous Goddesses around the world who are known for their connection to magic. Some Goddesses were known in antiquity as being the ally of witches, such as the Greek Hekate, whilst others have adopted that role in more recent times, like the Welsh Goddess, Cerridwen. Despite being one of the most magical of the Egyptian deities, Isis is not known as a 'witch Goddess'. Today, Isis is less often viewed as a skilled magician and instead her power is viewed as a type of divine omnipotence. Her ability to help her devotees, is perceived as an act of omnibenevolent maternal compassion, rather than the response of a talented magician. Perhaps this is because when Isis reached the Greek and Roman world, she was already viewed suspiciously, and so her magical aspects were overridden by maternal, healing qualities.

The narrative has thus far explained how Isis became great in her magic. The following chapters will illustrate how she consistently put this magic to use.

Chapter 2

Mythology: Death & Rebirth

The next section of Isis' story carries a multiplicity of meanings and great significance. The love between Isis and Osiris is iconic, destined from birth, united in bliss, and enduring beyond death. Here Isis demonstrates the strength of her character, the greatness of her power and the promise of eternal afterlife to humanity.

The Murder of a God

The previous chapter concluded its narrative with Isis and Nephthys raising Osiris' child together (one who was not in line for the throne). This was a much later addition to the story, adding a Greek flavour of scandalous drama. In Egyptian versions the story dictates that Isis and Osiris ruled together as strong, compassionate monarchs. Everyone was at peace. Everyone except Set, who was jealous of his eldest brother. The earliest sources of the myth tell that Osiris met an ambiguous untimely end, with no one specifically to blame. His death is treated as taboo. Old Kingdom references claim that Osiris "fell on his side", or collapsed dead at Abydos, the epicentre his cult centre in Middle Egypt (Hart, 2005). To depict something was to make it real; therefore, there are no ancient Egyptian scenes depicting how Osiris died. The details of his demise were of greater interest to much later Greek and Roman authors (Assmann, 2005; Hart, 2005). Nevertheless, it was of mythic necessity for Osiris to die, so that he could then be reborn and set the example for future kings to follow. By the Middle Kingdom, Set is named as the one responsible for his brother's death (Hart, 2005).

Nut and Geb's second-born son, Set, was a God who reigned over the realms of chaos, that which was foreign, the desert, raw minerals, and thunderstorms (Pinch, 2002). He was a dominant character brimming with feral masculinity and representing all that was 'other'. This was a stark contrast to his twin brother Osiris. Set was overcome with envy towards his brother and fixed his eyes upon usurping the throne for himself. He knew that the only way he could legitimately inherit this position, was if Osiris were to die before siring a legitimate heir. Isis and Osiris were known for their power over life, having provided the Egyptians with rich Nile floods and agricultural success. The chances of them failing to procreate was therefore unlikely. This contrasted greatly to Set and Nephthys, who had been allocated dominion over the barren desert lands and are not known to have sired any offspring together. Set would have to act quickly if he was to prevent an heir from being conceived.

The Greeks were not as squeamish as about the details of Osiris' murder as the Egyptians. Plutarch recorded how Set (who he names Typhon) plotted to kill Osiris. During a festival, Set presented the court with an elaborately decorated chest and challenged that whoever could fit inside perfectly would be proclaimed the winner and would be awarded the chest as a prize (McCabe, 2008). Guests took it in turns trying the chest out for size until eventually it was Osiris' turn. Playing the amicable host, Osiris laid himself down inside the chest like those before him. This time, however, the minions of Set rushed forward and sealed the lid tight, locking Osiris within. In cruel irony (or perhaps, perfect necessity) the God of the fecund Nile Valley was then cast into the river, left to drown in the currents inside the coffin-like chest. Just like that, Set was the next legitimate heir, and Isis, the now widowed queen, was in considerable trouble.

Isis Seeks the Body of Osiris

The chest, which was now a coffin containing Osiris' body was taken away by the river's current and lost to a grief-stricken Isis; however, rather than sitting in passive devastation, she took flight, determined to recover her lover's body. The stela of Amenmose records her sorrow as she searched for Osiris:

> *"Isis the powerful, protectress of her brother,*
> *Who sought him tirelessly,*
> *Who traversed this land in mourning*
> *And did not rest until she found him..."*
> (*Stela of Amenmose*; Assmann, 2005, p. 24):

Early accounts speak simply of how she found Osiris' body on the riverbank and "gathers up his flesh" (Hart, 2005, p. 117). Initially this may have been referring to her magically restoring his body from decomposition. The Greek's again told a more elaborate account of Isis' search. According to Plutarch, Isis' search led her to Byblos, an ancient city located in modern Lebanon, where she learned that the chest containing Osiris' body had been absorbed into a tamarisk tree. This tree had been cut down and used to build a wooden pillar within the royal palace. Unwilling to leave the pillar containing the chest, Isis chose to spend time in the palace at Byblos caring for the children of the royal court. During this time Isis became fond of the queen's infant son and decided to impart some of her magic to the boy. The spell involved burning the child in magical fire each evening, where he would grow more and more immortal. One night the queen walked in as the spell was happening and shrieked in terror at the sight of her magically burning child. Her cry disturbed the Goddess and the spell was broken. Isis was furious at the queen for ruining her spell and the boy's chance at becoming immortal. To make amends, Isis demanded to take the pillar back to Egypt with her, and of course the queen acquiesced (Plutarch, *Isis and Osiris* 14-17).

Upon securing the pillar containing her husband's coffin, Isis returned to Egypt, intending to keep it a secret from Set. In this instance, however, Set discovered what Isis had done and in a catharsis of rage tore Osiris' cadaver into fourteen pieces, scattering them across the land of Egypt. Despite this terrible turn of events, Isis once again refused to give up. She set off in search for the pieces of Osiris' dismembered body, honouring every place where a part was found as a tomb of Osiris (Lesko, 1999). Isis and her sister Nephthys magically transformed themselves into kites, and flew all over Egypt, searching for the pieces. The Goddesses may have been associated with this bird of prey because it hunted for carrion and the sound of its screeching was akin to the keening of grief:

"As the screecher comes, so the kite comes, namely Isis and Nephthys" (Bailleul-LeSuer, 2012, p. 134)

This plot is according to Plutarch's retelling of the myth in the fifth volume of his *Moralia,* entitled, *'Isis and Osiris'*. One additional notorious anecdote was shared by Diodorus Siculus in the first century BCE, reporting that the only part that remained unrecovered was the God's phallus, which had been thrown into the Nile. This was no deterrent to one such as Isis, who used her life-giving magic to fashion a replacement (McCabe, 2008).

Resurrection

As with his death, Isis' method for resurrecting Osiris varies with each telling. What remains consistent, however, is her magical approach. According to the *PT* her life-giving milk is an essential ingredient for his resurrection (Lesko, 1999). Another version describes how, having united Osiris' body parts upon a funerary bed, the Goddess enfolded Osiris within her feathery embrace and "created breath with her wings" (Lichtheim, 1976, p. 83). Nephthys, who had no part in her consort's violent intentions, assisted her sister in Osiris' resurrection. Both Goddesses are depicted as kites guarding the God's body during his funerary rites. As winged women they are also shown protecting other deities, such as Horus, or favoured deceased mortals (Bailleul-LeSuer, 2012). The image of one being sheltered between the wings of a Goddess became a potent representation of protection, no matter the name of the Goddess depicted.

Whilst the Egyptian sources are not, for the most part, structured in such a linear narrative, the next phase of the story is clearly illustrated in temple reliefs. Scenes of Osiris' funeral show him fully membered, with Isis and Nephthys mourning on either side of the funerary bed. With his body complete, and Osiris' life force returned, the couple took the opportunity to conceive an heir, so that the throne would no longer be compromised by Set's ambition. It is clear in Egyptian iconography that the conception occurs when Osiris is shown in mummy-form. This event is captured beautifully many times, with Isis hovering as a bird above the erect member of Osiris. One such depiction remains within the Temple of Seti I at Abydos.

Isis as a Kite above Osiris (Author's own image from Abydos)

This is contrary to Plutarch's version which dictates that Horus had already been born, prior to Osiris' death (Plutarch, *Isis and*

Osiris 18). Either way, this is great restorative magic on Isis' part. Following on from his resurrection, Osiris did not intend to return to the throne as a living king. Instead, he was the first being to be reborn into the afterlife. With the help of Anubis, Osiris was transformed into the first mummy and became the example for humanity to follow through identifying with him in their own funerary rites.

Goddess of Funerals

The first attestation of Isis' name appears in the 5th Dynasty in the mortuary context of the *PT* (Tower Hollis, 2009). These famous texts are amongst Egypt's earliest writings and were carved on the walls of royal tombs in Saqqara, northern Egypt (built before the Pyramids of Giza). The content comprises of spells (or 'utterances') to ensure that the king will be successfully reborn into the afterlife. They are so sophisticated that it is likely they were already well established before they were carved inside the pyramids (Malek, 2003). For this reason, it is reasonable to deduce that, although this is the earliest written evidence of a Goddess known as Aset, she must have been known by the elite before this date.

Originally, the God Osiris would have been responsible for the king's regeneration as the king adopted the form of Osiris himself. As time went on, however, it was Isis who took on the role of restoring Osiris to life and the king by association (Tower Hollis, 2009). The shift in regenerative power between Osiris and Isis, where Isis became the active giver of regeneration and Osiris the passive receiver of her magic, is reflected by her growing influence in other areas of religious ideology.

During the Old Kingdom it was believed that the Osiris-King would have ascended to the realm of the Imperishable Stars in the heavens. As the cults of Isis and Osiris became widespread amongst the common population in the New Kingdom, the focus shifted towards Osiris' reign in the underworld realm, known as the *duat* (Roberts, 2000). The gift of rebirth was originally a privilege reserved for the king and a select few who would serve him in the next life. Clearly then, the *PT* belonged to an inaccessible kind of magic, reserved for the select few. The Middle Kingdom *CT* and the New Kingdom *BD* (more accurately named *The Book of Going Forth by Day*; Ikram, 2003) granted more people instructions for entry into the afterlife. Furthermore, the transference of funerary texts onto objects, such as linens and papyri, meant that even more people could access this magic and be reborn themselves (Ikram, 2003). This is important because a wider audience of people could now access images and writings regarding Isis and Osiris. Despite this democratisation of the afterlife, it is true that it was still only available to those who could afford such funerary rites. Nevertheless, it was now *ideologically* possible for everyone to be reborn like Osiris.

For those who could afford a full mummification process, equipped with Canopic Jars, amulets and spells, there was a whole plethora of Gods to protect them. Isis and Nephthys were joined by Neith and Selket, who each watched over the Four Sons of Horus. These are the characters who are represented on the lids of canopic jars, protecting the four primary organs removed during mummification (Pinch, 2002). Thus, all these entities would watch over both the body and the soul in the afterlife.

Although Isis performed the central act of regenerative magic, she was supported by her twin sister Nephthys throughout. When Isis and Nephthys are depicted together the viewer can often identify each Goddess by the hieroglyphs upon their heads: Isis wore the throne sign and Nephthys (whose name, *Nebet-Hut* meant 'Lady of the House'), wore the hieroglyph of the palace (Ruether, R. et al, 2005); occasionally these signs appear beside the Goddesses, or upon on their person (Bailleul-LeSuer, 2012).

One Goddess is shown at the head end of the funerary bed, whilst the other kneeling at the foot end. It is only ever Isis who is shown flying in kite form directly above Osiris. During funerals, professional mourners act the part of Isis and Nephthys, keening over the dead who embodied Osiris. In a late text known as the, 'Stanzas of the Festival of the Two Kites,' from the *Bremner-Rhind Papyrus* (abbreviated hereafter, *BRP*) female mourners are adorned with wigs and recite hymns to Osiris (the deceased) to the accompaniment of tambourines. The Goddesses call out to Osiris, asking him to return to his body:

> *"The first-born in the womb of thy mother.*
> *O that thou wouldest come to us in thy former shape,*
> *That we might embrace thee, thou forsaking us not..."*
> (*BRP* 1:19-21)

The Goddesses grief is tangible in their cries:

> *"... And our eyes are weeping for thee,*
> *The tears burn.*
> *Woe (is us) since our Lord was parted from us!...*
> *... Draw nigh, so please you, to us;*
> *We miss life through lack of thee.*
> *Come thou in peace, O our Lord, that we may see thee..."*
> (*BRP* 3:2-4, 3:17-19)

It is clear how the story of Isis' grief and the resurrection of her lover was perceived as a very real narrative, which the Egyptians attempted to recreate upon the death of their own loved ones. The goal of rebirth and perpetual existence was the central aim of Egyptian life after death (Ikram, 2003). Isis held the key to this transformative magic and offered it to all who underwent the correct funerary rituals.

A Contemporary Pagan Perspective

To many, the murder and dismemberment of Osiris may seem like a brutal, evil act committed against a beneficent God by an aggressive, jealous one. The worship of Set became markedly less popular as time went on for two reasons. Firstly, the more popular Isis' cult became, the more troublesome Set's role in the mythology was perceived; secondly, by the end of the New Kingdom Egypt faced many threats from outside of Egypt. Set, being a deity of foreign lands, therefore, would have been distrusted (Wilkinson, 2003). Despite these developments, there are many Pagans today who recognise the divinity of Set and continue to worship him. When his actions are perceived within the context of the cycles of nature they may be better understood.

Osiris is the God of the Nile floodplain and the cycles of agriculture (Hart, 2005). He was the keeper of this necessary cycle of planting, growing, and harvesting, and as such he too had to follow the rules of nature and *ma'at*. Just as the fields are harvested and die, so must Osiris be born anew. This may be why it is significant that Osiris drowned in the Nile, with his body sent to the source of fertility. In viewing the cycle in this context, it may be possible to explain why Set went on to dismember him, scattering his parts like seeds across Egypt. According to Plutarch, a fish consumed Osiris' phallus (Plutarch, *Isis and Osiris* 18) which can be considered a clear sign of the river accepting this 'seed'. Ancient mummiform figures filled with corn seeds, known as corn-mummies, have been found in Egypt and are a manifestation of this idea of life within death (Constanza Centrone, 2004). This living and dying cycle and the sacrifice of one God by another is not so unlike the Western neo-Pagan mythology of the Oak and Holly Kings who battle at the summer and winter solstices (Farrar, & Farrar, 1984). This mythological cycle is a way of explaining the necessity of death, both in terms of agriculture and the earth, and in terms of our own existence. With this understanding, Set's contribution to the story need not be demonised by modern day Pagans.

Isian mythology is rooted in Egyptian experiences of life and landscape. This part of her story is a retelling of the Egyptian agricultural cycle. Its function was to teach the ancient Egyptians about the mysteries of birth, death and regeneration. For those of us today, living far from Egypt, it is important to understand what this agricultural year would have been like for an ancient Egyptian. This cycle dictated human survival every year in a very real life-determining way. A low flood or failed crops would result in malnutrition, disease and death. This cycle remains a challenging lifestyle for many people in parts of the globe today. For other readers of this book, such a life may be considerably different to their own. Isis' governance over nature may reflect other realities for them instead. Regardless, the fundamental truth of her story remains, that we all are born, live, and die, just like all other plants and animals. Wherever we live, Isis governs this cycle. By acknowledging this, we may begin to appreciate why Isis, who brought healing and rebirth, came to be known as a 'saviour' Goddess (Pinch, 2006).

Understanding Set's role in Osiris' necessary death may not alleviate the pain felt by Isis at the loss of her lover. For contemporary worshippers of Isis her pain cannot be ignored. Nevertheless, despite the sorrow she endures, Isis is one empowered by her own agency, who acted in the face of strife. Without Isis, Osiris would have remained dead within his watery coffin. Without Isis, his body would have remained lost and scattered across Egypt. It is through her magic that life is breathed back into him. It is through her body that his life-force is passed on through a successor. It is Isis who possesses the power to transform Osiris' death into life. With this power she is the promise of salvation to all people who fear what awaits us in the end.

This first section of her mythological story introduces a deep love between a divine couple and the violent betrayal of trust by their kin. It addresses the Goddess' desperation to find her beloved and longing for him to return to her. She carried his child in her womb, a child which would be in constant danger from his father's murderer. Already in the first half of her story it is easy to see why many people would have sympathised with her superlative struggles and believe that she, above of all Goddesses, would understand their own earthly heartaches and sorrows. She is a Goddess who truly empathises with our grief in times of loss, or betrayal. In addition to her compassion she offers the gift of rebirth, however we may interpret this. It is at this point in her story, the death, restoration and rebirth of her lover, that Isis expresses her important role as a vital funerary Goddess. But her story does not end here.

The mythology of Isis continues following the birth of her son, Horus and his battle for the throne. We have now seen how Isis achieved her status as one 'Great of Magic' and her role as a Goddess of funerals and rebirth. Now the story continues and we look upon her face as the Queen Mother.

Chapter 3

Mythology: Mother & Son

Isis is well-known as the mother of Horus, through extensive artistic depictions of her nursing him upon her lap. Horus' conception and rise to maturity is essential to Isis' mythology in overcoming the oppressive power of Set. Her care of him demonstrates, not only her maternal love, but also more of her magical abilities and cunning. Furthermore, it is as the (future) king's mother that we really appreciate Isis' role as a sovereign queen.

Who was Horus?

Egyptian mythology is filled with triads of Gods, typically consisting of a God, a Goddess and their divine offspring, although not exclusively. An example of this is the Memphite Triad comprising Ptah, Sekhmet and their child, Nefertem. Another triad consists of Khnumn and his two consorts Satis and Anuket, known as the Elephantine Triad. Most famous, however, is the triad of Isis, Osiris, and Horus (named Harpocrates by the Greeks; Pinch, 2000). Isis and Horus form the archetypal image of Divine Mother and Son and act as the prototype for living queens and royal heirs to imitate. In some ways it was more important for the future king (the living Horus) to emphasise his bond with his mother (the living Isis) than with his father (Hart, 2005). Isis was identified as Horus' mother from her very first attestation in the *PT*, before either were associated with Osiris in texts (Lesko, 1999). Historically speaking, Horus predates both of his mythological parents, in the form of Horus the Elder (*Heru-Wer*). Early on, Hathor was both the mother and the consort of Horus the Elder. It was later that he joined the Ennead as one of the brothers of Isis. This made him the uncle to Isis' son, Horus the younger (or, *Heru-sa-Aset*, Horus son of Isis). It is likely that the concept of *syncretism* brought these two forms of Horus together (Pinch, 2002). In basic terms this meant that one deity could merge with another deity to create a composite form where the powers of each were blended or expanded (Hornung, 1996).

The Mother of Egypt's Heir

Hathor appears in the historical record during the Old Kingdom 2nd Dynasty (2800-2650 BCE), hundreds of years before the first attestation of Isis. Hathor's Egyptian name, *Hut-Hor*, translates to 'Mansion of Horus'. This could refer to Hathor's maternal aspect, with her body being the literal home of the God for nine months (Wilkinson, 2003). Isis' Egyptian name, Aset, translated to 'throne'. She was the personification of the throne and royalty of Egypt. This is clearly shown in depictions of Isis with the infant heir, Horus, seated upon her lap, upon the throne of Egypt Herself. Isis is also shown as the mother of the historical kings. Sculptures and reliefs shown infant kings and upon their mother's laps, or suckling the cow Goddess, imitating Isis and Horus (Lesko, 1999).

Conception of Horus

Sources differ on which point in the story Horus was conceived. Native Egyptian sources record that the conception occurred concurrent with Osiris' regeneration, as seen in the hymn to Osiris from the stela of Amenmose:

> "*[Isis] Raised the weary one's inertness,*
> *Received the seed, bore the heir,*
> *Raised the child in solitude,*
> *His abode unknown.*"
> (*Stela of Amenmose*; Lichtheim, 1976, p. 83)

Here, Osiris is the 'weary one', whose weary 'inertness' is obviously the result of Set's brutal attack. One description in the *CT* refers to Isis' impregnation by means of a flash of lightning:

> *"The Lightning flash strikes, the gods are afraid,*
> *Isis wakes pregnant with the seed of her brother Osiris..."*
> (*CT* 148; Lesko, 1999, p. 162)

Other accounts describe and depict how with the movement of her wings, Isis wafts life-giving air back into the mummified form of her husband. Osiris' member is aroused and reaches up to Isis flying above him. This imagery was a way for Egyptian reliefs to infer intercourse between the deities, without being too explicit. Such scenes are shown again and again in religious art, from the temple of Abydos, to the roof chapel of Dendera (Wilkinson, 2000). Isis now carried the heir of Egypt within her womb, baring a lineage from Osiris, the earth God Geb, and the creator Ra-Atum:

> *"What he shall rule is this land, the heritage of his father Geb...*
> *I am Isis, one more spiritlike and august than the gods;*
> *the god is within this womb of mine and he is the seed of Osiris."*
> (*CT* 148; Gilula, 1971, p. 14)

In the Marshes

Isis knew that it was her son's destiny to avenge his father's death and defeat his usurper, Set. According to the *CT*, Ra-Atum, warned Isis to cover the pregnancy in secrecy, to avoid harm coming to her infant as she feared:

> *"If you are pregnant, then conceal this from the gods...*
> *and that the seed of Osiris is he, lest that enemy who slew his father*
> *shall come and break the egg in its early stages –*

the one of whom The Great-of-Magic is afraid."
(*CT* 148; Gilula, 1971, p. 14)

Under the protection of the seven scorpions of the Goddess Serqet, Isis heeded the Creator's advice and sought sanctuary in the Delta (Pinch, 2002). It was here, in the marshland of Chemmis, that Isis gave birth to Horus, hidden from the knowledge of Set (Lesko, 1999). Religious art depicts a bovine-Goddess, or a seated Isis, nursing the infant God amongst the marshy reeds.

Isis and Horus in the Marshes (Author's own image from Philae)

Here she kept his existence secret and did all she could to care for him. Isis' ability to protect her infant son was a comfort to human women, afraid of birth and premature infant death. The Goddess is described attending common births and in *Papyrus Westcar* she attends the birth of a prince. In this papyrus, Isis and three other Goddesses, along with the God Khnum attend the king's wife, Ruddjedet, during her birth of triplets:

Then Isis placed herself before her, Nephthys behind her, and Heqet was hastening the birth...

Then Meskhenet approach[ed] him and said 'A king who will perform the kingship in this entire land!'

And Khnum made his body healthy..."

(*Papyrus Westcar* 7-8, 10, 12-14; Nederhof, 2008, pp. 43-45)

Interestingly, the position of Isis and Nephthys are strikingly similar to the position guarding the body of the deceased. Perhaps this is a reference to the dangers of ancient childbirth and the Goddesses' role in delivering life to death and death to life.

The idyll of the young God and his mother living in the fecund marshes of the Delta was a short lived one. Despite the initial protection offered by Serqet's scorpions, Horus was not indefinitely safe from harm; on the contrary, the Egyptians were most aware of infant vulnerability to disease, malnutrition, and venomous animal bites. This is perhaps where the magic of Isis became most significant to the daily life of Egyptian people. Numerous spells record how, as an infant, Horus was on the receiving end of venomous bites from serpents and scorpions. The Late Period *Metternich Stela* reveals a vulnerable side to Isis, where she is like any human mother, afraid for her young child's survival (Scott, 1951; Pinch, 2006; Metropolitan Museum of Art, Stela 50.85). The text talks of how she seeks the help of local women for a cure. The God of knowledge and wisdom, Thoth, came forward when the local women were unable to provide Isis with the answers she needed. Thoth proffered his advice on the matter, teaching Isis how to save Horus. Isis goes on to use this newfound knowledge to heal mortal children in similar danger, proclaiming:

"Every reptile with stings listens to me... Isis, great of magic before the gods, has spoken, to whom Geb has given his magic to repulse

poison."
(Scott, 1951, pp. 210-211)

This demonstrates how Isis is a Goddess constantly learning her craft and developing her magical skills. In other texts Isis heals Horus without assistance. Perhaps this balance of vulnerability and power is a deliberate demonstration of Isis' complete character. She is a mother, fearful for her child's safety, but also a skilled magician. Her followers could connect to her through her empathy and rely on her magical competence. Isis' impressive healing abilities were demonstrated through the healing of the Sun God and the resurrection of Osiris. The promise of rebirth was unquestionably important to the ancient Egyptians, however, it was Isis' role as a healer during life was crucial to the general population. Childbirth and infancy were dangerous times of human life. Isis took agency and was able to use her magic to heal her son, which offered a promise to her followers that they could imitate the Goddess and do the same in times of affliction.

The Contendings of Horus and Set

The stories relating to the *Contendings of Horus and Set* record the inevitable next phase of the narrative. The narrative attempts to answer important questions about patriarchal inheritance and who is truly next in line. The living king of Egypt identified with Horus, having inherited his throne from his deceased father. This mythic cycle affirmed his right to rule, when other contenders may have presented a challenge. And so, it goes that Isis raised Horus to manhood in secrecy until it was time for him to challenge Osiris' usurper and killer. The stela of Amenmose provides us with further details in the narrative, recording the moment when Isis proudly introduces Horus to the court of the Gods:

"[Isis] Who suckled the child in solitude, no one knew where,
Who brought him, when his arm was strong,
Into the hall of Geb – the Ennead rejoiced:
'Welcome, Osiris' son,
Horus, stout of heart, justified,
Son of Isis, heir of Osiris.'"
(*Stela of Amenmose*; Assman, 2005, pp. 24-25)

Unfortunately, Horus' claim to the throne was not as straight forward as Isis might have hoped. According to the New Kingdom *Papyrus Chester Beatty* (abbreviated hereafter, *PCB*), Set refused to relinquish his claim. For the next eighty years the pair quarrelled before the Gods, necessitating them to take sides on the matter (*PCB* 3:1). Not everyone in the Divine Court agreed that Horus' claim was as obviously legitimate as Isis believed; for example, Pre-Harakhti (a form of Ra), favoured Set for his superior age and virile nature, believing that Horus was juvenile and incapable of fulfilling such an important office:

"You are despicable in your person, and this office is too much for you, you lad..."
(*PCB* 3:8; Kelly Simpson, 2003, p. 94 (after Broze, M. 1996)

To resolve the matter, the Gods appealed to the Goddess Neith, who spoke in favour of Horus and recommended that Set be given two Semitic Goddesses, Anat and Astarte, as wives in compensation (*PCB* 3:4-5); alas, this still did not satisfy Ra. There was no other choice but for Horus and Set to prove their claims through a series of battles and challenges. Set had brute strength and experience on his side. Horus possessed the strength of a young warrior and the benefit of a powerful magician as an ally. Isis was determined to use her magic to ensure that her son succeeded to the throne and that Osiris' and her own suffering was avenged.

Isis had expected Horus to be accepted as the rightful king without question. Indignant that this was not so, she spoke loudly during the proceeding discussions. Set would not tolerate her protestations and demanded that the court be moved to an island away from her. He instructed the God Nemty to prevent Isis from crossing the river and reaching them. Of course, such a demand would never work for a shapeshifter such as she. Isis disguised herself as an old woman, tricking Nemty and paying her passage with a signet ring. Upon approaching the court of Gods, Isis next transformed herself into a beautiful young woman, distracting Set from his plotting. Losing himself in the presence of her beauty, Isis used her cunning to perform another trick: with her clever words, she told a story about a cattle-farmer's son whose inheritance had been stolen by another. She managed to convince Set to agree with her, that this was a wrong-doing and by doing so, he accidentally agreed that he was guilty of wrong-doing as well. At this, even Ra had to concede that Set had admitted to his own guilt (*PCB* 5:3-7, 5:12).

The only way to crown the true king of Egypt was to compete for it. One challenge involved the pair transforming into hippopotami and fighting one another whilst submerged for three months. This narrative is described in detail at Horus' temple in Edfu, recording the *Festival of Victory*. During this festival a ritual drama would have taken place, re-enacting the battle of the two Gods, with Horus destroying Set. Such is depicted in a wonderful relief showing Set in the form of a miniature scaled hippopotamus; depicting him thus would minimise his power in real life. During the ritual drama, priests would have destroyed small hippopotamus-formed models of Set as an act of sympathetic magic (Wilkinson, 2003).

Returning to *PCB*'s retelling, further troubles arise. Isis was sure that Horus would not survive Set's attacks below water. Attempting to prevent this, she cast a harpoon towards Set, accidentally spearing Horus instead. She tried again and this time succeeded in her aim; however, Isis was overcome with compassion for Set and withdrew the weapon. In a frustrated rage Horus recovered enough to remove his mother's head clean off her shoulders (PCB 8:9-9:10) Isis is quickly healed by Thoth, who replaces her head with that of the Divine Cow. This incident shows Isis in a humanised light as she makes mistakes and doubts herself. It also reflects her enduring compassion, mercy, and ability to forgive.

Whilst unsuccessful in helping her son during this last episode, Isis makes up for it in the next challenge. Again, it is a competition between physical dominance and cunning. This section of the myth is continued in the above papyrus but also in earlier fragments from the Middle Kingdom *Kahun Papyrus* (Pinch, 2002). In this episode Set attempted to sexually dominate Horus in order to prove his superiority. Isis predicted Set's intentions and urged Horus to prevent this, advising him to catch Set's semen in his hands without his knowledge (Pinch, 2002). Horus heeded this advice and after the encounter, he returned with Set's seed cupped within his hands. Isis cried out loud at Set's offence and cut off her son's soiled hands, casting them away at once. Of course, she magically restored them as she had with Osiris' severed body. Beating Set at his own game, Isis had Horus spread his own semen onto some lettuces for Set's unknowing consumption (PCB 11:5-11:11). The following day Set stood before the court of Gods and boasted:

"I have performed a man's work against him [Horus]*."*
(PCB 12:4; Kelly Simpson, 2003, p. 99 (after Broze, M. 1996)

It is clear that, at least in a Middle and New Kingdom mythological context, the submissive partner in a male homosexual liaison was perceived less favourably, and so the Gods were horrified by this proclamation against Horus. However, Horus confidently denied Set's claim and so the wise God Thoth decided to call forth each Gods' seed in order to prove who dominated who. Due to Isis' cleverness, the seed of Set was nowhere to be seen; on the other hand, the seed of Horus emerges from within the belly of Set (*PCB* 12:5-13:1). Set is humiliated and refused to let the matter go. One more trial occurs after this, though it is unclear from the text what it was exactly. Regardless of its outcome, the Gods have grown tired and (finally) agree that Osiris, in his role as Divine Judge in the afterlife, may be called forth to announce his successor. Of course, Set stands no chance. After being restrained in chains, Set was forced to relinquish his claim and Horus ascended to the throne (*PCB* 13:5-16:2).

This story reflects a very important debate over royal succession, asking who is a more legitimate heir, the deceased king's mature brother, or his young son? The matter is further complicated by a fusion of myths, where Horus (the Elder) was the brother of Osiris and Set (as illustrated in chapter 1). The Egyptian words for family members were limited to father, mother, sister and brother (Faulkner, 1962), making distinctions of inheritance unclear in texts, as the translation below confirms:

"*Thoth then let out a loud cry, saying, "Is the office to be awarded to a maternal uncle even while a bodily son is still about?*

Then said Banebdjede, the great living god, "Is the office to be awarded to the lad even while Seth, his elder brother, is still about?"
(PCB 4:8-9)

Perhaps 'elder brother' was synonymous with uncle? Or was Horus the Elder being referred to in a mythic fusion? Regardless, as the succession was unclear the pair had to fight for the throne. The dichotomy of these two Gods is in fact much older than the first attestation of Isis. Horus and Set are known from at least the Early Dynastic Period as dual protectors of Egypt (Wilkinson, 2003). This was before Set bore the negative associations that came from murdering Horus' father. Once Set was forced to relinquish his claim to the throne, he returned to this protective role, using his strength against the chaos serpent Apep and protecting Ra in the heavens (Pinch, 2002).

A Contemporary Pagan Perspective

The story of Horus and Set's sexual competitiveness may at first seem like a rather strange one, but from a contemporary Pagan perspective the creative magic represented by semen might be obvious. On the one hand, the story could be concerning physical dominance, considering the sexual dominant as superior. The response from the Gods does indeed confirm this view, with how they sneer at Horus, believing he submitted to Set; however, today we can choose to look at the story through a contemporary western lens, avoiding projections of sexual judgement. The right to the throne in this case is based on paternal inheritance. Each God is asserting their superior claim by the strength of their paternal link – which is *symbolised* by their semen. Whose semen is connected more strongly to the predecessor, a brother or a son?

What of Isis' role in this part of the story? Firstly, the ambiguity over succession should be answered by the very definition of Isis' name. Isis as the Throne Goddess very clearly seats Horus as the heir upon her lap – not Set. The question of succession is because the story focuses on father-son inheritance. If we observe the maternal line instead, then the heir could not be doubted. Some scholars have indeed suggested that royal succession had more to do with the king's mother, and instead was matrilineal (Tyldesley, 2006).

Despite the above, Ra was still unhappy with Horus inheriting the throne instead of Set. Isis therefore needed to intervene to ensure her son's success. The narrative provides key insights into Isis' character and abilities, such as her determined and active approach to ensure Horus succeeded. We see more of her shapeshifting and regenerative magic. She was not always successful in her attempts to help Horus, showing a vulnerable side we can identify with. As with any mother, Isis was not infallible. We all make mistakes. She also expressed compassion towards Set, her ultimate enemy, when she saw how he suffered at her spear. Despite some errors in her judgement, Isis' cunning magic spares Horus' dignity and allows him to gain the upper hand from Set. Ultimately, she achieves her goals, demonstrating how brains can overcome brawn.

As witnessed from her trickery with Ra and how she used shapeshifting to sneak past Nemty, Isis is not opposed to using cunning to achieve her goals. In contemporary Wiccan magic, it is often recommended that magic be used to harm none; however, perhaps Isis teaches us that there are blurred lines in magic and that it is sometimes permissible to use our subjective view when using it? As expressed previously, the use of magic in a morally ambiguous fashion may not be what one initially expects from a Goddess. Regardless, Egyptian magic is neither black or white, good or bad. Isis is a Goddess who upholds the balance of *ma'at* and uses her Divine Judgement to ascertain what is best.

* * *

This narrative is rather long for an Egyptian myth and concludes the main mythic storyline of Isis, Horus, and Osiris (although more side stories are certainly told). These three chapters have addressed the Isian mythic cycle: 1) Isis is born of Nut and Geb, sister and wife to Osiris, 2) The pair rule in Egypt and teach the Egyptians the secrets of agriculture, 3) Osiris is murdered and Isis goes in search for his body, twice, 4) Isis restores Osiris to life and conceives Horus, 5) Isis raises Horus in the marshes and protects him against worldly dangers, 6) Horus is presented to the Gods to compete for the throne and Isis offers her assistance in this, 7) until finally Horus is crowned king and Osiris is avenged.

Chapter 4

Isis of 10,000 Names

From earth, sea, and sky, to life, death, and magic, Isis' powers became all encompassing. During the Graeco-Roman Period, starting in 332 BCE, Mediterranean culture flooded Egypt, bringing its Gods to Egypt and taking Egyptian Gods across the sea. The Greeks and Romans who travelled to Egypt interpreted Egyptian religion through their own eyes, thus merging and assimilating cultural ideas (Stadler, 2017). It is during this time that Isis underwent transformations which are recognisable to how we view her today (Bowden, 2010). The Greeks and Romans attributed new areas of influence and symbols to Isis, leading her to gain more and more epithets, until she was thus-named Isis *myrionymos,* or Isis of innumerable names (McCabe, 2007). At the height of this period there was little beyond her divine sphere of influence.

From Solar to Lunar

One of the major transformations that Isis underwent through Graeco-Roman eyes is a transition from being a solar Goddess to becoming a lunar Goddess. Throughout Egyptian history Isis shared very important iconography and aspects with Hathor, the Egyptian Goddess of love, motherhood, and the sun. Hathor received a widespread cult and was a beloved deity by royalty and commoners alike. One reason for this was her multifaceted nature which appealed to all kinds of people and led her to be identified with almost any other Egyptian and foreign Goddess (Wilkinson, 2003). By the New Kingdom, Isis' cult had risen in prominence and she adopted Hathor's horned sun-disk headdress and various aspects of the Hathorian cult (Tower Hollis, 2009). At times both Goddesses are shown together, each offering their own powers to the scene. A famous painted relief from the tomb of Queen Nefertari shows the pair standing identically on either side of the queen, greeting her in the afterlife (Tyldesley, 2006). The Goddesses could look so alike that it would be impossible to identify which Goddess was being represented, unless she was accompanied by her name in hieroglyphs. Such is the case for many pieces of modern art depicting the pair.

Isis was not just borrowing Hathor's iconography without cause, for she too was a solar Goddess. It has been noted in a previous chapter that Isis' connection to afterlife rebirth reflected the solar cycle. From the *PT* the rising, setting, and re-rising of the sun each day was reminiscent of what to expect at death. When the sun set behind the western mountain, effectively dying, he would travel through the Otherworld, the *duat*, illuminating that place for the duration of his stay, before being reborn at dawn, shining upon the earth the next day (Roberts, 1995). It was therefore entirely appropriate that the Goddess of mourning and funerals was connected to the solar cycle. Not only did Isis bring Osiris back to life, as the sun returns each dawn, but she gave birth to Horus, who in his avian form, became a solar sky God. Horus' eyes were said to be the sun and the moon (Pinch, 2002). Isis is therefore the mother of a sun God.

Adding further to this solar theme, Isis wore the image of the cobra, the *uraeus*, at her brow. This rearing cobra represented the Sun Goddess and identified her as an Eye of Ra (Roberts, 1995). Hathor, Sekhmet, and Tefnut were primarily identified with the uraeus, poised ready to spit fiery venom at the enemies of their father, Ra. By wearing the uraeus, Isis also embodied this. In some depictions Isis took the form of a serpent, often as a composite image of woman-serpent-kite (a woman's head and serpent body with the wings of a kite). In the form of a winged serpent, Isis fulfilled an apotropaic role, possessing the fiery solar power to administer harm to enemies, as well as the ability to offer protection to the vulnerable beneath her wings.

It is, then, clear that in the original ancient Egyptian perspective, Isis had solar connotations which were significantly emphasised through her similarities with the great solar Goddess Hathor; however, despite this, as her popularity grew during the Graeco-Roman period and spread across the Mediterranean, Isis was transformed into a lunar Goddess.

To the Greeks and Romans, the sun was interpreted as masculine, and the moon as feminine:

"Theia brought forth great Helios
and shining Selene
The Sun and the Moon..."
(Hesiod, *Theogony* 371-373)

The Greeks and Romans projected their concept of the divine feminine as lunar onto Isis. As a result, associations which were linked to the moon, were also attached to her. Numerous reliefs and sculptures from this time depict Isis crowned by the lunar crescent and indeed Apuleius' description of Isis confirms this:

"I had hardly closed my eyes when suddenly from the midst of the sea a divine face emerged... above her forehead, a flat round disc like a mirror - or rather a symbol for the moon – glistened with white light."
(Apuleius, *Met* 11:3)

The horned headdress was originally understood by the Egyptians to represent the celestial cow Goddess, who lifted the sun God between her horns and carried him up to the heavens (Pinch, G. 2002). These horns were re-interpreted by Greeks and Romans as imitating the shape of the crescent moon:

"...they put horns on her (Isis') head both because of the appearance which she has to the eye when the moon is crescent-shaped and because among the Egyptians a cow is regarded as sacred to her." (Diodoros Siculus, 1st Century BCE; Delia, 1998, p. 543)

Therefore, Isis became a lunar Goddess, fulfilling Greek expectations of the divine feminine and serving other functions that her Mediterranean devotees sought from her, as below.

Goddess of the Sea & Water

It is very likely that the moon's obvious connection to the tides and bodies of water contributed to Isis' newfound dominion over the sea. Despite being attached to a coastline, Egypt did not have a native sea divinity and only later adopted Gods such as the Canaanite Yam, to fulfil this function (Wilkinson, 2003). The Nile was of greater importance to the Egyptians before this point. The river's annual flood was more important than the sea, as it re-fertilised the land for new crops and marked the growth of food and valuable resources. The flood waters were also associated with the death of the drowned God, Osiris:

"The canals fill, the rivers flood, and with the cleansing that comes from Osiris." (PT 455; Allen, 2015, p. 115)

The flood-time was heralded by the celestial rise of the star Sothis (Sirius), personified by the Goddess Sopdet, later associated with Isis (Pinch, 2002). It was believed that Isis-Sopdet would take to the heavens to announce the coming of the flood and the drowning of Osiris. This gives further credence to the aforementioned idea that Osiris' death was connected to the life-giving powers of the Nile. Due to Isis' connection to the flood she was credited for nurturing the whole land and its people with the fertile silt that washed ashore:

"She is the one who pours out the inundation,
Which makes all people live and green plants grow."
(*Inscription from the Temple of Philae*, Žabkar, 1983, p.134)

Naval navigation was not of primary importance to the Egyptians, but it certainly was for the Greeks and Romans. When they adopted Isis as equal protector of the great and the humble, who herself had travelled across the Mediterranean Sea with her worshippers, it seemed natural to call upon Isis for safety during naval voyages. The previously mentioned quote from Apuleius describes Isis emerging from the sea, crowned by the moon. In this role, the Greeks knew her as Isis *Pelagia*, who watched over those who travelled by sea. This is clearly demonstrated by the famous Pharos Lighthouse in the Graeco-Egyptian coastal city of Alexandria, which was dedicated to Isis *Pharia* (Stevenson et al., 1889). As Isis *Pharia*, she is shown wearing a cloak which imitated a sail, clearly identifying her as the driving force guiding ships across the waves (Donalson, 2003). Previously Isis had fronted the solar barque of Ra as one of his divine protectors. During this late period, she protected mortal sailors too, bringing ships safely back to harbour (Pinch, 2002).

Identification with Egyptian Goddesses

Isis and Hathor are two of the most comparable Egyptian deities. As detailed throughout this book so far, Isis shared Hathor's iconography as a solar-mother Goddess. Hathor was also the patron of music and dance, and instruments played a central part in her cult, especially the sistrum rattle. The sistrum was so connected to Hathor that countless examples exist of sistra decorated with her bovine features (Wilkinson, 2003). Sistra were connected to the cults of many Gods, however, for it was a key ritual component in Egyptian religion from as early as the Old Kingdom. Priests would have played sistra as an offering to the Gods, to pacify their anger and please them. Sistra were particularly popular within the Roman period cult of Isis where they became an iconic aspect of her festive processions:

> *"Then the crowds of those initiated into the divine mysteries came pouring in, men and women of every rank and age... All together made a shrill ringing sound with their sistrums of bronze and silver, and even gold."*
> (Apuleius, *Met* 11:10)

Both Hathor and Isis looked after pregnant women, those in childbirth, and young infants. Their care over the dead, and celestial aspects further connected them with the Star Goddess Nut. All three are known interchangeably as Tree Goddesses. The Tree Goddess possessed maternal attributes and offered sustenance and refuge to the dead (Buhl, 1947). As Marie-Louise Buhl points out, the Egyptians expected that the needs of the dead mirrored the needs of the living; therefore, these protectresses of the dead took the form of a tree, offering the deceased shade from the sun and refreshing liquid libations (Buhl, 1947). One of the earliest images of this Goddess was in the form of a sycamore fig with arms suckling King Thutmose III (Lesko, 1999). This image conjures up a connection to Isis nurturing Horus on her knee and is meant to show how the king is sustained by the milk of the Goddess herself. As time went by, the Tree Goddess became more and more anthropomorphic; first as a woman whose legs morphed into a tree trunk, then into a woman who stood in front of the tree.

The shared association of a Tree Goddess was just one way in which Isis and her mother Nut were connected. The Goddess Nut was the primordial mother of the Ennead, mother of Isis, and Goddess of the stars in the sky. She was the embodiment of the sky itself, shown in art as a giant, star-spangled woman, arching over the earth. Isis' role as a star Goddess, in the form of Isis-Sopdet, naturally aligned her with Nut celestial qualities.

They were also connected through their care for the dead. Those who successfully passed through to the afterlife would dwell in the land of the *duat*, located within Nut's starry body. Many coffins were decorated with Nut or Isis inside the lid, arching over the cadaver in a protective embrace (Buhl, 1947). Images of a winged Nut on the outside of coffins are virtually impossible to differentiate from Isis' iconography, especially when both Goddesses had a central role in protecting the deceased and enfolding them in a winged embrace.

Isis was also associated with Ma'at, Goddess of truth and balance (Pinch, 2002). The verb *maa* in Egyptian was written with an eye hieroglyph and meant 'to see', alluding to this Goddess's ability to see the truth of all things. As a concept, *ma'at* also meant balance in the universe and was the opposite of chaos. The Goddess was winged and her sacred feather was used on the scales of judgement in the afterlife. If one's heart was heavier than the feather of Ma'at, then the individual was deemed unworthy of the afterlife and died a second death (Pinch, 2002). Ma'at's attribute as a defender of justice and order, of discerning truth and fairness, and judging the dead, made her similar to Isis. Egyptian theology allowed for each of the Gods and Goddesses to be connected to one another in some way and saw no contradiction in using their epithets and names interchangeably.

Identification with Foreign Goddesses

The introductory chapter of this book featured a quote from the *Met* whereby Isis states that she is the manifestation of all gods and goddesses. The text goes into further detail by listing specific Goddesses with whom Isis is identified:

> *"My divinity is one, worshipped by all the world under different forms, with various rites, and by manifold names. In one place the Phrygians, first-born of men, call me Pessinuntine Mother of*

the Gods, in another the autochthonous people of Attica call me
Cecropian Minerva, in another the sea-washed Cyprians call me
Paphian Venus; to the arrow-bearing Cretans I am Dictynna Diana,
to the trilingual Sicilians Ortygian Prosperpina, to the ancient
people of Eleusis Attic Ceres; some call me Juno, some Bellona,
others Hecate, and still others Rhamnusia; the people of the two
Ethiopias, who are lighted by the first rays of the Sun-God as he
rises each day, and the Egyptians, who are strong in ancient lore,
worship me with the rites that are truly mine and call me by my real
name, which is Queen Isis." (Apuleius, *Met* 11:5)

Here, the author, Apuleius, shares a Roman understanding of
Isis, as that of a Universal Goddess, recognisable in all other
divinities. A characteristic feature of Roman religion was the
process of *interpretation romana*, that is appropriating foreign
concepts and adapting them to fit Roman requirements (Smith,
2010). The Romans were able to do this with many different
cultures, such as the Etruscan, Greek and Egyptian, adding to
their sense of religious antiquity. This way of interpreting the
Gods is something commonly found in polytheistic cultures,
where similarities between deities can lead to their translation as
one and the same (Assmann, 2008). Such a practice was already
old by the time of Apuleius. When Herodotus observed Egyptian
culture in the 5th century BCE, he was under the opinion that the
Gods of Greece had originated in Egypt and travelled to Greece
and elsewhere under new names and disguises (Assmann, 2008).
Isis fits into this theological view perfectly. Her mythology and
character possessed so many different aspects that she naturally
shared similarities with a multitude of other deities; thus, she
became a universal cosmic deity, sovereign over all.

In addition to embodying a universal nature, Isis was
identified with several specific foreign Goddesses, including
several within a single pantheon.

Isis & Demeter-Ceres

Isis' connection to the flood and the growing of crops in Egypt was one reason for why she could be equated with the Greek grain mother Goddess, Demeter (and the Roman, Ceres). Herodotus identified Isis with Demeter and Osiris with the Greek God of wine, Dionysus; this is echoed by the Roman writer Diodorus Siculus much later in the first century BCE (Bowden, 2010). Adding another century on to this, and Isis' association with Demeter-Ceres was still circulating, with Plutarch weaving the two Goddesses' stories together. Indeed, the mythology surrounding these Goddesses share some poignant similarities. Firstly, each Goddess is associated with agriculture and the grain harvest. By the Roman period, Egypt was the breadbasket of Rome. Therefore, Egypt's main commodity, and its most famous Goddess, Isis, were combined and associated with the Roman Goddess of grain, Ceres and the Greek Demeter (Peacock, 2003).

"...you are bountiful Ceres, the primal mother of crops..." (Apuleius, *Met* 11:2).

A second association that Isis and Demeter-Ceres share, as often follows agricultural Goddesses of provision, is their strong maternal aspect. Both Goddesses were Divine Mothers. We already know that Isis was traditionally shown in *lactans*-iconography, that is, breast-feeding her infant son (Higgins, 2012); Demeter's mythology centred upon her relationship with her daughter, the maiden Goddess of spring, Kore. In fact, the myth of Demeter and Kore, leads to her third similarity with Isis: loss and despair. The Eleusinian mysteries related to the mythic cycle of Demeter and Kore, centring on Kore's abduction by Hades and her mother's despair at her loss. In her grief, Demeter starved the earth of green life until her daughter was returned to her from the realm of the dead.

When Kore did return it was as Queen Persephone (Roman Proserpine), who was contracted to spend half the year on the green earth and the other half in the Underworld. Whilst not the ideal situation, Demeter was overjoyed at the reunion and restored life to the earth, creating the annual cycle of seasons (Homer, *Hymn to Demeter*). Not only does this myth remind us of Isis' loss and desperate search for her beloved, but it also attempts to explain the agricultural seasons, as with the death and rebirth of Osiris. Therefore, Demeter's three mythic themes, grain, motherhood, and loss, were mirrored by Isis and vice versa.

Homer's *Hymn to Demeter*, features a segment of the story, where Demeter visited the palace of King Celeus and Queen Metanira, in Eleusis (Homer, *Hymn to Demeter* 210-270). Here, she disguised herself as an old woman and agreed to nurse the couple's sons, whereupon she took favour on one particular son, Demophoön. Demeter decided that she would give the boy the gift of immortality, through the means of magic fire; however, one night the boy's mother broke the spell, walking in on the scene and screaming in terror at the sight of her flaming child (Homer, *Hymn to Demeter* 250). This will sound familiar as such a tale has already been shared in chapter 2. Hundreds of years after Homer's hymn was written, Plutarch rewrote this story through the eyes of Isis in his *Isis and Osiris*. Instead of Eleusis, Isis stayed in Byblos; instead of looking for her lost child, she searched for the body of Osiris (Plutarch, *Isis and Osiris* 18). It is obvious here that Plutarch was identifying the two Goddesses with one another by conflating their stories.

Other Graeco-Roman Associations

In addition to the association with Demeter-Ceres, images of Isis identify her with Fortuna, where she is shown carrying a sheath of wheat or a cornucopia (Donalson, 2003).

Isis-Fortuna (J. Paul Getty Museum, 71.AB.180)

By the Late Period, Isis adopted Hathor's cow iconography, which perhaps inspired her Graeco-Roman identification with Io, a mythical woman who fell under the unfortunate gaze and lust of the Roman God Jupiter (Greek Zeus). According to Hyginus in 2nd Century CE, Jupiter attempted to hide Io from Juno (Greek Hera) by transfiguring her into a cow (Swetnam-Burland, 2015). The stories vary on whether Io was a devotee of Isis, or whether she became divinised as the Goddess herself, but certainly the two were connected.

Isis was so absorbed into Roman religion that in addition to merging with Ceres, Isis often appeared conflated with the mother of Rome herself, Venus (Swetnam-Burland, 2002). In Pompeii, a hot spot of Isis worship, Isis was accompanied with statuettes of Venus Anadoymene, where devotees appear to have worshipped the two in conjunction (Hackworth Peterson, 2016). Venus Anadoymene was depicted as a beautiful semi-nude woman wringing out her hair after a bath. The exotic beauty of Isis was embodied by the famous Queen Cleopatra VII, who proclaimed herself the living image of Isis and was often depicted with the sensual allure of Isis-Aphrodite (Al Shafei, 2016). One inscription describes a priest of Isis-Aphrodite, attesting to a syncretised form receiving formal cult (Jones, 2017). Their connection is not surprising, given how both Goddesses were believed to offer safety to those travelling by sea.

In Byblos, a city in modern Lebanon, a temple was dedicated to Isis, in her local form of Astarte (Wilkinson, 2003), which in turn could arguably link her to further Eastern Goddesses, such as Ishtar and Inanna. And so on.

A Contemporary Pagan Perspective

With the dawn of Catholic Christianity many ancient Goddesses found a way to survive in the form of the Christian Virgin Mary. Some scholars have argued that the imagery of Isis nursing Horus was adopted into the Christian iconography of the Madonna and Child (Higgins, 2012). Others may see a parallel today between the two, with Isis mourning her sacrificed love, whose rebirth and male heir promised hope for humankind, and with Mary's grief over her own son's martyrdom for humanity. As modern-day Pagans, we can trace this familiar pattern and see how Isis found a way to survive in a changing world that was intent to destroy her memory. Perhaps we can look upon these new interpretations, not with scorn for a stolen history, but instead with a smile for a kind of posterity? Some will, some will not.

Contemporary Pagans hold varied views on the multiplicity of deities. For a strict polytheist, it may seem impossible to view the Egyptian Aset as one and the same with the Graeco-Roman Isis. The form of Isis surviving today is indeed almost unrecognisable from the Old Kingdom Egyptian version. However, for soft polytheists or monolatrists, this transformation of a Goddess and her identification with other Goddesses, may be entirely reasonable. Therefore, the historical journey recounted here is one of a developing mythology across time and cultures. The nature of the characters involved remains up to personal gnosis.

Chapter 5

Temples & Cults

Outstanding records of Isis' cult survive, dating between the 4th century BCE to the final closure of Egypt's last remaining temple, the Temple of Isis at Philae, after the coming of Christianity 550 CE. Despite Her common appearances in texts and temples across Egypt and the Mediterranean, it wasn't until the 30th Dynasty (380-343 BCE) that temples were dedicated primarily to Isis (Pinch, 2006; Wilkinson, 2003). Isis' cult became popular in Egypt and across the Mediterranean following centuries of foreign occupation. When the Macedonian Alexander the Great conquered Persian rulers in Egypt, he approached the native culture with an attitude of respect and reverence. Emancipation from Persian rule may have led the Egyptians to feel a renewed desire to reclaim national identity and religious expression (Bowden, 2010). The rulers of the Ptolemaic Dynasty, following on from Alexander, were increasingly reliant on Rome for diplomatic support, resulting in Egypt growing more and more cosmopolitan. This is important because the spread of Egyptian Gods had originally been a political affair, rather than one based on migrating personal piety; now the Gods were travelling with ordinary people to new homes abroad (Bowden, 2010).

Egyptian Temples

Egyptian temples were not for common worship, like other religious buildings we may be accustomed to in the West today. The temples were houses for the Gods and access was restricted to members of the priesthood. By the New Kingdom, the priesthood was more formally organised and only certain priests would be permitted entry into the holy of holies, the inner sanctuary of the God. This would be dependent on their role and required a certain level of ritual 'purity' (Wilkinson, 2000). The style of Egyptian temples changed over the thousands of years of Egyptian history; however, New Kingdom and Graeco-Roman temples are most familiar to us today due to their higher state of survival. Most temples comprised of a protective enclosure wall, fronted by two pylons guarding the entrance to an open courtyard. Beyond the courtyard there would have been an hypostyle hall, filled with decorated columns and a series of chambers. Towards the back or centre was the inner sanctuary/ies of the deity. As one got closer to the deity's shrine the ceiling would have become lower and the space would have grown darker, creating a primeval and mysterious atmosphere (Wilkinson, 2000).

The only time common people would have interacted with the temple was outside of it, during festival days. Festivals provided opportunities for the wider populace to glimpse the icons of the Gods which were usually hidden in their sanctuaries. Non-clerical Egyptians would have worshipped their Gods and communed with their ancestors within the home, rather than in a sanctified temple. Perhaps, it can be argued that the place where Isis received the most cult worship, was within people's homes, much like how contemporary Pagans worship today.

Egypt: Temple of Isis, Philae

As mentioned above, temples dedicated solely to Isis arose in the 30th Dynasty. For any pilgrims seeking sacred sites of Isis, the Temple of Philae, located close to Aswan in the south, is the prime place to visit. Due to flooding caused by the building of the Aswan High Dam, the temple of Philae Island was successfully relocated by UNESCO in 1980 to Agilkia Island, in order to preserve it (UNESCO website, 'Philae, Egypt'). Although it is not in its original location, the complex maintains its ancient integrity and I feel it still holds its sacred essence. High foliate pillars stretch across the colonnade and provide shade from the

African sun; kittens and cats play and prowl along the paths; birds chirp amongst the pink flowers adorning the trees. A sense of mystery is elevated through the experience of approaching the island by ferry, sailing upon the Nile and viewing the columns of Trajan's Kiosk draw nearer.

Trajan's Kiosk (Author's own image from Philae)

Where other sites in Egypt may hold a more touristic, or abandoned feel, those protecting and visiting Philae temple seem to respect the sanctity of the space to this day. The first shrine on the original island dates to the Late Period, during Taharqo's reign (690-664 BCE), though the surviving complex dates to the reign of Nectanebo I (380-343 BCE). This temple was dedicated primarily to Isis, although other deities shared her space, such as Horus, Hathor, a couple of Nubian deities and the deified emperor Augustus (Wilkinson, 2000). The temple is famous for being the last place of Pagan worship in Egypt, surviving deep into Christianisation until the reign of Justinian in 550 CE (Wilkinson, 2000). This extraordinary survival was perhaps down to the temple's location far south and is a testament to the conviction of Isis' followers.

Egypt: Temple of Isis, *Behbeit el-Hagar*

Also dating to the end of the Late Period, a Temple of Isis was located in the delta at *Behbeit el-Hagar,* ancient Busiris, home to the 30th Dynasty kings (Wilkinson, 2000). These rulers were particularly dedicated to Isis and were the ones responsible for the rise in the number of Isis temples in Egypt. Sadly, the temple now lies in ruin close to the river, as the result of earthquake damage. What remains are piles of rubble in the centre of the village, amongst which column tops with Hathor's enigmatically peaceful face can be spotted. For the romantic historian such a site can hold tendrils of magic still.

Egypt: Temple of Hathor, Dendera

The Goddess Hathor had more temples dedicated to her than any other Goddess in Egypt and Isis often makes an appearance in them. The temple of Dendera is an exceptionally well-preserved example of a roofed temple from the Ptolemaic period (Wilkinson, 2000). Occupied as early as the Old Kingdom, the temple was dedicated to Hathor in the Middle Kingdom and continued to be developed into the Roman Period. Isis appears in multiple reliefs throughout the complex and is sometimes only distinguishable from Hathor herself, by the hieroglyph upon her horned headdress.

Isis at Dendera (Author's own image from Dendera)

The Temple of Hathor at Dendera is famous for its exquisite interior decoration, particularly upon its ceilings. Here the journey of the stars and the hours of day and night are personified. The temple was home to the Dendera zodiac, which once adorned the roof chapel and is now preserved in the Louvre in Paris (Wilkinson, 2000). A scene of Isis in kite form reviving Osiris, with the support of Nephthys can still be seen within this chapel. Isis has her own dedicated space in the complex, in a temple annexe beside the dried-out sacred lake. This small temple was dedicated to the Birth of Isis and would have once housed a tripartite statue of Isis and Nephthys supporting Osiris (Wilkinson, 2000).

Egypt: Temple of Osiris, Abydos

Another temple of great significance to Isis is of course the Temple of Seti I at Abydos. King Seti I dedicated this temple to Osiris in the New Kingdom (1292-1189 BCE). The city of Abydos dates right back to the Early Dynastic period of Egypt, at least, and was first sacred to the chthonic god Khentiamentiu, meaning 'foremost of the Westerners (the dead)'. By the Middle Kingdom's 12th Dynasty Osiris had taken on this epithet and a nearby Early Dynastic pharaonic tomb (3000-2890 BCE) was believed to be the location of his tomb. This religious significance is why Osiris' main festival was hosted in Abydos (Wilkinson, 2000). The temple contains a row of seven chapels, each dedicated to Ptah, Re-Horakhty, Amun, Osiris, Isis, Horus, and the deified Seti I (Wilkinson, 2000). Isis' chapel is decorated with many images of her in anthropomorphic form, standing and sitting in reception of offerings from the king (Calverley, et al. 1933). On the northern wall her sacred barge can be seen, with the Goddess' aegis placed at the prow and rear, crowned with the horned sun-disk (Calverley, et al. 1933, pl. 18, 19). Each of these chapels within the temple contain a false door, except from Osiris' which leads into further chambers. This false door would have acted as a portal for the deity to pass in and out of the chapel (Wilkinson, 2000). The Temple of Osiris in Abydos can be considered an important place for Isis worship, not only because of the inclusion of an Isis chapel there, but also because the cult of Osiris and his resurrection relied upon Isis' intervention. The festival of the Mysteries of Osiris which took part in Abydos, featured Isis in all its proceedings. The pair were not to be separated.

This temple has survived extraordinarily well, with its roof still intact. It is relatively dark, save for mysterious shafts of light which pierce through the halls. Song-birds nest on top of the pillars and the space carries an atmosphere of sombre tomb-like reverence, balanced with the feeling of hope that we will see our lost loved ones again... Finally, the Osirion, Osiris' mythological tomb, is truly a place for peaceful reflection. Although no longer subterranean and now exposed to the sun, the flooded area glows green like the skin of Osiris and quietness falls upon the stones. One may be able to sense Isis watching over the holy remains of her beloved as the pilgrim peers down.

Egypt: Temple of Horus, Edfu

The Temple of Horus at Edfu, far in the south of Egypt, commemorates Horus' victory over Set, his ascension to the throne and his union with the Goddess Hathor. Naturally, Isis features in numerous reliefs as a key player in Horus' narrative. An important space that she specifically occupies is a special area known as the temple *mammisi*. Such structures are an interesting feature of all major Graeco-Roman Egyptian temples and are known as the 'place of giving birth'. As such, they celebrated divine marriage and royal birth, honouring the divine mothers Hathor and Isis, and their sons Horus and Ihy (Kockelmann, 2011). Offerings of milk would be given here for the protection and nourishment of the Gods (Daumas, 1958). Whilst divine birth was the central focus of a *mammisi*, the king's connection to the gods - as the embodiment of the divine son Horus himself - is also an important aspect of these temples (Wilkinson, 2000). The purpose of these rituals was to re-enact divine and royal birth each year, maintaining legitimacy and ensuring continuation. Beautiful scenes remain, showing the Goddesses Isis and Hathor nursing the divine child amongst marshy foliage (Wilkinson, 2000). The *mammisi* of Edfu is one of the most well preserved, though others can be found at the Temple of Philae and the Temple of Dendera (Wilkinson, 2000).

Other Egyptian Cult Centres

Isis had a presence in chapels and temples throughout ancient Egyptian history, stretching the entire expanse of the Nile. In Lower Egypt (the north), during the Middle Kingdom Isis and Bast were considered the patron Goddesses of the region known as the Heliopolitan nome, which is located around modern-day Cairo. The pair also received cult together at a Karnak shrine, in Middle Egypt, Luxor. Isis' worship from this time is also attested in areas such as Akhmim and further south in Hierkonpolis, Edfu, and Coptos (Lesko, 1999). In the New Kingdom she shared sacred space with Horus at his temple in Buhen, where she was called the Mistress of Nubia (modern day Sudan; Lesko, 1999). Most temples dedicated to Hathor – there are many! – will also feature Isis in some way.

Mediterranean Mystery Cults

By the time the cult of Isis gained popularity and began to spread across the Mediterranean, it had taken the form of a mystery cult. The term 'Mystery Cult' refers to traditions whose community have been initiated and obtained secrets withheld from non-initiates (Bowden, 2010). Perhaps one reason the worship of Isis in the Mediterranean achieved Mystery Cult status, was because the inner workings of Egyptian cults were secretive and kept separate from the public eye. This must have been interpreted as a clear indicator of a mystery tradition, which was recognised in their Greek and Roman mystery cults. The Romans were especially perturbed and fascinated with Egyptian religion. Despite clear Romanisation, the cult of Isis maintained much of its Egyptian identity and as such it was not always received in a positive light. In 28 BCE Octavian forbade the worship of Isis within Rome and the emperor Tiberius repressed many foreign cults, going to the extent of burning related religious paraphernalia (Suetonius, *Tiberius* 36; Jones, 2017). Temples of Isis came as quickly as they went, according to the persuasions of the current emperor (Jones, 2017). The Romans adopted exotic Egyptian ideas but were not so interested in the lives of the Egyptian's themselves and therefore did not appreciate the religion in its original context (Swetnam-Burland, 2002).

Despite distrust by certain emperors, the cult of Isis is an excellent example of a Graeco-Roman mystery cult with surviving evidence of its festive observances and its initiates' acts of personal piety. Not all cults of Isis abroad were Mystery Cults, however, and unlike the Egyptian temples, Greek and Roman worshippers were permitted access to the Goddess's shrine for her worship. A follower of Isis was known as an Isiac (plural Isiasci) and her temples were called Iseums (Bowden, 2010).

Greece

Although geographically in Egypt, the coastal port of Alexandria was culturally a Greek city (Lloyd, 2003) and was a centre for the worship of Isis and the Egypto-Hellenic God Serapis (Wilkinson, 2003). Greek travellers were also taking the Goddess home with them, from this city and across the Mediterranean Sea. A Greek inscription from Athens dating to 333 BCE records the earliest attestation of an Iseum in Greece. The inscription details a request to build a shrine to Aphrodite, "just as the Egyptians had founded a shrine of Isis" (*Inscriptions Graecae II, 1, 337* 40-

45; Jones, 2017). Five hundred years later another Greek text by Pausanias records that there was a shrine of Isis in Tithorea, close to Mount Parnassus. Entry to this shrine was restricted to those whom Isis had invited herself through dreams. The shrine held such cult superstition that the consequence of entering it without initiation or permission, would be to witness a ghostly haunting and die of fright (Pausanias, *Description of Greece* 10.32:13, 17; Jones, 2017). The writer goes on to describe a three-day festival that took place at there every spring and autumn. During this time the shrine would be cleansed according to secret rituals, old offerings buried, and traders would set up stalls outside. The festival culminated in a procession and a ritual sacrifice (Pausanias, *Description of Greece* 10.32:15-17; Jones, 2017). What the festival celebrated is unclear, although due to the spring and autumn dates, it is plausible that it related to a Hellenised version of the seasonal cycle of Isis and Serapis.

Italy

There is no evidence for an official Isis cult in the city of Rome before 43 BCE, though her cult is certainly attested elsewhere in what is now modern-day Italy (Bowden, 2010). Originally dating to 100 BCE, Pompeii's Temple of Isis is one of the earliest sanctuaries dedicated to an Egyptian deity in Italy (Swetnam-Burland, 2015). Columns outline the rectangular circumference of the temple and a traditional Roman exterior altar remains. Such altars would have been the focus of ritual sacrifices for the gathered public. The temple is raised on a platform, reached by a short flight of steps, within which an interior altar would be based (Scheid, 2003). The temple is decorated with numerous paintings, which remain preserved to this day due to the otherwise fatal eruption of Mount Vesuvius in 79 CE. These paintings reveal how local followers of Isis, the Isiasci, understood the myth of Isis and Osiris (Bowden, 2010). Another fresco from the Temple of Isis in Herculaneum around 62-79 CE depicts an Isiasci ritual in action (now kept in the Museo archaeologico nazionale di Napoli).

In it we see worshippers dressed in white, forming two rows either side of traditional Egyptian shaven-headed priests. A flautist is seated, playing music, as a priest reads from a manuscript and another tends to a central fire amongst gathered devotees. This scene provides a tantalising look into what such rituals could have looked like.

Once initiated into the mystery cult of Isis, the initiate was expected to maintain a service to the Goddess in some way, unlike other cults which held no such obligations (Bowden, 2010). Following Isis was a joyful, yet no less serious business. It appears to be a very different kind of cult from the ecstatic mayhem of the Dionysian mysteries. Despite very much behaving as a mystery cult requiring initiation, it appears that through following proper procedures, anyone who devoutly wished to dedicate themselves would be permitted to do so, and thus the cult of Isis was by no means an exclusive club. Such a concept would contradict the very nature of Isis who was saviour to all. Indeed, not all cults of Isis even involved an initiatory element (Bowden, 2010). Whilst the mystery cults were a popular phenomenon, they were just one manifestation of the cult of Isis. Isis also had priests serving her in other cities and temples in much the same way as any other deity.

Other Temples

Worship of Isis is attested in numerous other locations across the Mediterranean and beyond. For example, there is evidence of an Egyptian cult of Isis and Serapis in the port city of Ephesus (modern Turkey). Here, an inscription was found describing two local sailors observing a festival of Isis blessing the ships (Walters, 1995). This suggests that people in Ephesus were observing the Roman ship festival dedicated to Isis, the *navigium Isidis* (chapter 6). There is also evidence of Isis' worship as far as

Britain, such as a small statuette found in Thornborough, (Green, 1983, pl.X) and an altar stone in London, which mentions the rebuilding of an Isis Temple (now in the Museum of London, no. 77.57; Merrifield, 1983). This incredible geographic journey is the credit of travelling merchants, politicians and armies. It shows how much Isis meant to her followers, that they would bring her name, image and stories with them on their travels.

A Contemporary Pagan Perspective

In addition to hundreds of Egyptian pilgrimage opportunities offered by tourist companies, New Age, and contemporary Pagan travellers, there are several modern temples dedicated to Isis today. One such temple is the exquisite Temple of Isis, located with the Isis Oasis retreat centre, California, USA. At this modern temple, Isis' universal nature is revered:

> *"We honor the Goddess Isis, who in modern terms equates with Mother Earth, and has been worshiped longer than any other deity known on the planet. We refer to Her as Isis of 10,000 Names, as she has many incarnations in other religions and practices all over the world."*
>
> (Isis Oasis website, 2020)

The temple is a legally recognised place of worship and is decorated with neo-Egyptian motifs. It is truly remarkable that a Goddess whose worship first appears 4500 years ago in North Africa, has people creating temples and altars devoted to her in the USA, UK, Ireland and Western Europe today! There is nothing quite like visiting the ancient temples and sites themselves; however, worshipping in these spaces is not always easy.

One is often interrupted by disapproving stares or reprimands from guards, especially when *Baksheesh*, or tips cannot be offered. This is not unique to Egypt (which is otherwise a very welcoming country)! Many heritage sites around the world are not yet open-minded about spiritual visitors or outward expressions of spiritual practices at sites. I can see this changing in the future as scholars and heritage professionals are beginning to consider the benefits of a mutually beneficial dialogue between themselves and special interest groups (i.e. Pagans), though this may take some time yet. Whilst singing in procession to the ancient temples would be wonderful for some of us, one may have an equally spiritual experience walking in reverent silence amongst the ancient pillars.

Travelling to Egypt is not within the means of many people. Fortunately, we live at a time where distances are shortened by the accessibility of information. We can listen to the sounds of Egypt through reconstructed music online. We can talk to others from all over the world about our interests. We can consume books and articles galore and we can create our own shrines to Isis, even if just in our living rooms! Ancient devotees of Isis may never have set foot in Egypt, just as common ancient Egyptians may never have set foot in a temple. They nevertheless worshipped her with all their hearts and felt her love reach back. Pilgrimage is special, but it begins within. By reading this book, you have already made a kind of pilgrimage closer to Isis.

Chapter 6

Festivals & Rituals

Festivals were a key feature of state religion in ancient Egypt and were a way for the people to acknowledge important mythic cycles throughout the year. They were an opportunity for the people to catch a glimpse of a deity's icon outside of their sanctuaries, as well as a chance to have some festive fun. All festivals would have contained ritual elements, some public and some private within the temple itself. A ritual is a set of repeated actions, which in this context are done for a religious purpose. By this definition an annual festival itself is one big ritual.

Wep Ronpet & the Rising of Sirius

By the Ptolemaic period the rising of Sirius in the heavens, heralding the arrival of the Nile flood in August, was interpreted as a manifestation of Isis-Sopdet (Wilkinson, 2003). The rising of Sirius was a cause for celebration because it indicated the start of a new agricultural year, just as the rebirth of Osiris promised returning life. The year was thought to have comprised of 360 days, with five epagomenal days added on thanks to the God Thoth winning them from the moon God Khonsu. The Goddess Nut gave birth to her children on these days five days, which ended in the new year festival, *wep ronpet*. As described in the introduction of this book, Isis was born on the fourth day. The rising of Sirius coincided with the festival marking Isis' birth, making it a very special time to celebrate her. As should be clear by now, worshipping Isis was a matter of accepting duality: celebrating life came with honouring death, and vice versa. Therefore, there was also a more sombre association with the rising of the Nile: Osiris' death in its waters. In the *BRP* Isis claims to have flooded the land with her tears:

"...I desire to see thee!
I am thy sister Isis, the desire of thine heart,
(Yearning) after thy love whilst thou are far away;
I flood this land (with tears?) to-day..."
(BRP 3:13-16)

Thus, Isis was believed to have risen in the sky in kite form to search for Osiris in the Nile, which she caused to overflow with her tears. The flood brought life, as well as death. This story was still being told by Egyptians almost two centuries later, as recorded by the Greek Pausanias:

"...the Egyptians hold a feast of Isis when they say that she is mourning Osiris. At that time the Nile begins to rise and many of the natives have a saying that the tears of Isis make the river rise and water the fields."
(Pausanias, *Description of Greece* 10.32:18; Jones, 2017)

The festival mentioned by Pausanias links the rising of the flood, with another festival, the Mysteries of Osiris.

The Mysteries of Osiris & Ritual Dramas

Attested from the Middle Kingdom, the festival known as the Mysteries of Osiris took place in the season of *Khoiak,* when the flood had passed and crops began to grow (Teeter, 2011). This was celebrated country-wide, not only because of its popularity, but also because mythologically Osiris' body had been scattered across Egypt. Multiple towns could boast having housed his divine body. Ritual dramas and processions were a central part of state religion and this festival comprised of both. Parts of the mysteries were open to the public and other parts remained secret to the priesthood. The main location for this festival was Abydos, the legendary burial site of Osiris and his primary cult centre. First there was a public ritual drama, re-enacting the myth of Osiris' death and rebirth through Isis' magic. This was then followed by a public procession of Osiris' cult statue through the temple complex and surrounding cemeteries - which were already hundreds of years old by this point (Wilkinson, 2000). A statue of the God, Wepwawet, guardian of graveyards, led the way to Osiris' tomb, with the public following to join in a funerary rite (Teeter, 2011). Whilst members of the public were witnesses to this event, they were by no means passive. Devotees would create corn mummies representing Osiris' regenerative powers and often kept them a year before burying them in the earth. This practice of creating mummiform figures extended right through to the Roman period, growing more and more elaborate with time (Teeter, 2011).

The *BRP* records a long hymn to be spoken within the temple, away from the public gaze. The hymn's rubric specifies that it is to be recited during 'The Festival of the Two Kites,' taking place on the 22nd-26th day of the fourth month of the inundation, *Khoiak* (*BRP* 1:1-2). This date is the same recorded for the Mysteries of Osiris, and therefore was either an alternative name, or a coinciding observance. The 'Two Kites' in question, are of course Isis and Nephthys. The hymn records the Goddesses' song of mourning, crying over the loss of Osiris and beseeching him to return to them. We are fortunate to have access to this papyrus now, which would have otherwise been restricted for the eyes of literate lector priests and those taking part in the ritual. The rubric explains how the ritual is to take place:

"The entire temple shall be sanctified, and there shall be brought in [two] women pure of body and virgin, with the hair of their bodies removed, their heads adorned with wigs... tambourines in their hands, and their names inscribed on their arms, to wit Isis and Nephthys, and they shall sing from the stanzas of this book in the presence of this god." (BRP 1:2-5)

Though the festival above focuses on Osiris as the central figure, Isis is clearly essential to the rituals and festivities. Any festival dedicated to the Mysteries of Osiris may be considered a festival dedicated to the mysteries of Isis also. For without Isis, Osiris would have no resurrection and rebirth. There would be no mysteries at all, without Isis. This was understood by her Roman cults, who obviously placed the Goddess at the centre of their observance of the Mysteries, known to them as the *inventio Osiridis.* This Roman version of the festival also re-enacted the Isis-Osiris story, annually around the end of October (Hackworth Peterson, 2016).

The Festival of Lamps

Another festival along the same theme above, is attested by Herodotus in the 5th Century BCE and appears hundreds of years later in the 1st century CE Roman Calendar of Philocalus. It was known to Herodotus as the 'Festival of Lamps' and to Philocalus as the *Lychnapasia,* the 'Festival of Light,' or the 'Birthday of Isis' (Herodotus, *The Histories Vol.2* 62; trans. Godley, 1920; Salem, 1937, p. 166). Instead of emphasising the rebirth mysteries, this festival acknowledged Isis' *search* for her beloved. The Egyptian festival was adopted into the Roman calendar to correspond with the birth date of Isis, at the start of August (Salem, 1937). As with the celebration of the rising of Sirius, this was in time for the Nile flood, when Osiris was said to drown. Herodotus describes the Egyptians observing this festival in the town of Sais, in the Delta. In his famous and thoroughly entertaining (albeit sensational) work, *The Histories,* he describes the following:

> *"When they assemble at Sais, on the night of the sacrifice, they all keep lamps burning in the open air round their houses. These lamps are... burning all night. This is called the Feast of Lamps."*
> (Herodotus, *The Histories, vol. 2: 62*)

Herodotus claims that, in Egypt, this festival was second only to the one in Busiris, which was also related to the Festival of Lamps. This festival, however, culminated in a special sacrifice and its tone was one of lament:

> *"There, after the sacrifice, all the men and women lament, in countless numbers..."*
> (Herodotus, *The Histories, vol.* 2: 59, 61)

Navigium Isidis & Ritual Procession

Although the above festivals all focus on Osiris' death and Isis' grief, it is important to appreciate that this was not necessarily a sombre occasion (though at times it was). The cult of Isis and Osiris was one of hope for the continuation of life. Not all festivals of Isis were focused on this aspect of her worship, however. Beyond this mythic cycle, the Roman's marked another occasion in honour of Isis' beneficent influence over their lives, that of the previously mentioned *navigium Isidis*, or *Isidis navigium*. Every year on the 5th March devotees would invoke Isis to bless the ships at the start of sailing season, asking for successful trading ventures and for sailors to return home safely (Hackworth Peterson, 2016). In the *Met*, Isis herself says to Lucius:

> *"...when the winter's tempests are lulled and the ocean's storm-blown waves are calmed, my priests dedicate an untried keel to the now navigable sea and consecrate it as the first fruits of voyaging."*
> (Apuleius, *Met* 11:5)

The text continues to provide a detailed account of the festive proceedings, with many people joining in a, "special procession of the saviour goddess" (Apuleius, *Met* 11:9). During this procession, initiated devotees were recognisable from other attendees due to their all-white dress, with the women's hair bound and the men's heads shaven (Apuleius, *Met* 11:10). The procession was led by torches and lamplights, with participants carrying symbols of the Gods, and musicians playing pipe and shaking sistra. The Gods themselves joined the processional retinue, "deigning to walk with human feet," (Apuleius, *Met* 11:11) or being carried through their idols by priests. The procession led attendees to the seashore, where the icons were set down and a priest consecrated a ship, offering it to the sea:

> *"He took a lighted torch, an egg, and sulphur, uttered prayers of great solemnity with reverent lips, and purified the ship thoroughly, naming it and dedicating it to the goddess...*
>
> *When the ship was laden with generous gifts and auspicious sacrifices, it was untied from its anchor-ropes and offered to the sea..."*
> (Apuleius, *Met* 11:16)

Once the ship was out of sight, attendees processed back to the shrine.

Ritual processions were a common aspect of Egyptian festivals and rituals. One such procession occurred during the 'Festival of the Beautiful Union,' where Hathor of Dendera 'visited' Horus at his temple in Edfu, and vice versa. This visit is depicted clearly in Edfu itself, with reliefs showing Nile boats decorated with the aegis of each deity travelling towards one another (Verner, 2012). During the Mysteries of Osiris festival, a funerary procession to the God's burial place took place. Funerary processions were common for wealthy Egyptian families, where professional mourners played the roles of Isis and Nephthys for the deceased (Ikram, 2003).

Initiation into the Mysteries

In order to access a sense of belonging and the secret teachings of the Isis mystery cult, the devotee would need to undergo initiation. Of course, due to its restricted nature we have little information regarding what this involved exactly, although scholars have made educated guesses. Bowden (2010) postulates that it may have involved the would-be initiate spending time in a subterranean chamber, reminiscent of Osiris' tomb, re-creating the death-rebirth narrative. Such crypts have been discovered in temples such as the Temple of Isis of Gortyn, Crete, dating to the 3rd-2nd Century CE (Bowden, 2010).

In Apuleius' *Met,* the writer provides an account of one man's journey through the initiations of Isis. Though a work of fiction, some have suggested that the text provides true insights into Isiasci rituals, based on potential experiences that Apuleius observed as an initiate himself (Takács, 2008). We can attempt to draw together the process of Lucius' initiation, for the potential truths it may hold, keeping in mind the fictional integrity of the text all the same. According to the story, before initiation took place, the would-be initiate, Lucius, slept within the temple precinct and repeatedly received visionary dreams. He spent time here carefully considering his choice to initiate, for it would require demanding obligations, such as abstinence (Apuleius, *Met* 11.19). Upon awaking the initiate bathed and received purification from a priest, before commencing a period of ten days, during which no meat or wine could be consumed. Unlike Egyptian temples and in keeping with Graeco-Roman ones, every initiate was permitted entry into the inner sanctuary of the Goddess (Apuleius, *Met* 11.17). The first stage of initiation took the form of a symbolic death with prayers to Isis for salvation:

"both the gates of death and the guardianship of life were in the goddess's hands, and the act of initiation was performed in the manner of voluntary death and salvation obtained by favour."
(Apuleius, *Met* 11:21)

After the initiation took place, Lucius was shown texts written in hieroglyphic script that he could not understand, harking back to Isis' Egyptian origins. In the story he undergoes a second, undescribed stage of initiation, before the third stage pertaining to the essential mysteries of Osiris (Takács, 2008). Devotees and initiates appear to have been clad in white linens, and men had their heads shaved. Lucius goes on to the third stage of initiation in order to become not only an initiate, but a priest. The picture created above and in other areas of the text bare close similarities to the images depicted centuries before on the Herculaneum fresco. Therefore, at worse Apuleius was writing based on older material; at best he was recording a continuation of tradition, based on his own observances. What is clear is that although the mystery cults were a Mediterranean interpretation of Isis, they maintained intentional Egyptian markers and to some degree, becoming a part of Isis' cult involved embracing an Egyptian identity (Bowden, 2010). This should not be considered a barrier, however, for the cult was open to all and this identity was apparently not closed off by individual origins. As far as discovering what the initiates specifically learnt of the Mysteries of Isis, we are none the wiser. The text provided by Apuleius only features what would have been common knowledge, which is in keeping with Apuleius' own loyalty to the initiatory system (Takács, 2008).

The Daily Offering Ritual

Within the inner sanctuary of each temple a purified priest would have been responsible for completing an offering ritual to the deity, three times daily. This ritual has survived since the *PT* of the Old Kingdom and continued throughout Egyptian history (Teeter, 2011). It has been preserved through evidence of formal state religion, rather than the religion of the common people. At the centre of every cult was the icon, believed to be the physical home of the deity. To depict something made it real and so a deity's icon was a real manifestation and needed to be cared for as such. The ritual is performed thusly (Teeter, 2011):

1. At dawn the priest washed themselves in clean water and natron salt, before being fumigated with incense.
2. Before entering the sanctuary, the priest spoke prayers, lighting a lamp and incense. The *PT* offers a prayer for such a ritual, this time offering to the deceased King Unis:

"The fire is laid, the fire shines;
The incense is laid on the fire, the incense shines.
Thy fragrance comes to king Unis, O Incense;
The fragrance of king Unis come to thee, O Incense.
Thy fragrance comes to king Unis, O ye gods;
The fragrance of king Unis come to you, O ye gods.
King Unis is with you, ye gods;
Ye are with king Unis, ye gods..."
(PT 376-8; trans. Breasted, 2010, p. 126)

3. Upon entering the inner sanctuary, the priest would awaken the deity, opening the shrine doors and kissing the ground at her feet:

"Awake in peace! May your awakening be peaceful!"
(Meeks et al. 1999, p. 127)

4. Sand was poured on the ground and the icon was placed upon it following more liturgical prayers.
5. The icon was then cleansed of the previous night's ritual, by removing fabrics, jewellery and cosmetics. Once cleansed, the priest could begin to reapply these things afresh.
6. Once prepared for the day ahead, the icon would be presented with offerings of food, drink and flowers.
7. To close the ritual the priest would return the icon to its shrine and exit the sanctuary backwards, sweeping his or her footprints away as they went.

This would have been repeated every day at midday and sunset, though the latter two would have been less elaborate than the morning ceremony. If one wanted to recreate this ceremony today it is worth remembering that the common people may not have owned an icon at all, or at least one large enough to extensively dress and adorn. Furthermore, they would not have read from liturgical texts or had access to a separate shrine room. For the common Egyptian practicing domestic worship of the Goddess Isis, it is more likely that a lamp and incense would be lit and offered to a crude clay sculpture, along with offerings from the home and prayers from the heart. Isis was a Goddess of the people and would have been accustomed to rituals of grandeur as well as humble offerings of home-made bread and improvised prayers.

A Contemporary Pagan Perspective

Those observing the ancient Egyptian festivals and seasons in the southern hemisphere (SH) are more likely to be celebrating closer to the original Egyptian dates. Those in the northern hemisphere (NH) would experience them in reverse. For example, the Mysteries of Osiris during *Khoiak* would have occurred around October time. For the Egyptians this time was for growing vegetation; for us in the NH it is a time of coming darkness and cold. There are two ways to approach this: Firstly, one can choose to observe the festival later in March, during springtime. Secondly, one could observe the festival in October, aligning with the themes of death that arise during modern Pagan observances such as Samhain. Alternatively, one may choose to do both, with each season marking a different emphasis, as suggested below.

A Proposed Festival Calendar

Provided here, are two proposed festival calendars for the contemporary Pagan. It must be noted that unlike seasonal stories belonging to traditions such as in Wicca, this version does not always follow a linear narrative. I have also omitted exact dates and included only the month, for these festivals are based on natural observances and are therefore flexible. Whilst the Egyptian mythic landscape is specific to Egypt, I believe the myths can be brought to life through these festivals and can be adapted to each devotee's own context. For them to have any personal meaning, it is essential that one adapts it to reflect their own lands seasonal cycles and lifestyles.

Neo-Pagan Wheel of the Year

August (NH) / February (SH) – *The Birthday of Isis. The sacrifice of Osiris to the Land.* A chance to celebrate Isis' birth and to consider Osiris' necessary 'sacrifice' to the earth.

September (NH) / March (SH) – *Isis goes in search for the body of Osiris.* A festival of lamp light as the dark times approach.

October/November (NH) / April/May (SH)– *The Funeral of Osiris.* Ritual drama, re-enacting the funeral of Osiris and mourning Isis' loss.

December/Midwinter (NH) / June/Midsummer (SH) – *The Birth of Horus.* Isis gives birth to the Sun God. The promise of returning order and light is born.

February (NH) / August (SH) – *Isis nurses Horus, hidden in the marshes.* Life is starting to return to the earth, as Isis cares for the juvenile Sun God.

March (NH) / September (SH) – *Celebration of Osiris' resurrection.* The earth returns to life, just as Isis returned Osiris to life.

April/May (NH) / October/November (SH) – *Union of Isis and*

Osiris. Celebrating the *Hieros Gamos* of Isis and Osiris.

June/Midsummer (NH) / December/Midsummer (SH) – *The Contendings of Horus and Set.* Horus has come to maturity and risen as the glorious Sun God to avenge his father.

Ancient Egyptian Dates

August – *Wep Ronpet.* To celebrate the five epagomenal days before the new agricultural year. Day four marks the birthday of the Goddess Isis.

August – *The Festival of Lamps.* Isis rises in the heavens as Sirius and floods the land with her tears. This is marked by candlelit processions, seeking Osiris' body.

October/November – *The Mysteries of Osiris I,* and *The Festival of the Two Kites I.* To mourn the death Osiris and hold his funeral through sacred drama.

February (21st) – *The Festival of Victory.* Horus finally defeats Set and ascends to the throne (Blackman & Fairman, 1942).

March (5th) – *Navigium Isidis.* To mark the opening of sailing season, asking Isis to bless us with safety and abundance.

March – *The Mysteries of Osiris II,* and *The Festival of the Two Kites I.* A repeat of the former festivals of these names, but with the emphasis on Osiris' resurrection.

Chapter 7

Magic & Prayers

The Egyptian concept for the power of magic, *heka,* was described in chapter 1. *Heka* is a force running through all things, which one can harness to create changes in the world. Any prayers and rituals to Isis will involve her magic. Prayers may ask Isis to use her magic to help the applicant, as opposed to the magician or priest using their own magic, or the magic around them to cause change by themselves. For the modern practitioner, Isis is a Goddess great in magical ability and is ideal to call upon for assistance and wisdom.

Egyptian Magical Techniques

Egyptian magical spells are often presented in a bipartite or tripartite form: first there is an explanation or rubric, followed by actions to be done, then words to be said (Pinch, 2003). Most Egyptian spells deal with tending to poisonous bites and healing illnesses and wounds; therefore, many may not be as useful to the modern reader as the phone number for emergency services!

Spells took place at a specific time and day and required ritual purity before they could begin (Pinch, 2006). One key technique used in Egyptian magic was for the magician to embody the deity they were invoking the aid of. Such a proclamation is provided in a spell calling upon Isis to cure victims of poisonous bites (*Metternich Stela* 210-211; Ritner, 2008). Modern practitioners of magic and devotees of Isis may use this statement at the start of their own magical workings. Not only do we have a translation of this text, but Robert Ritner has provided a transcription from the original Egyptian in his work, *The Mechanics of Ancient Egyptian Magical Practice* (2008). From this, I have developed a pronunciation guide below so that readers may pronounce this statement in approximated ancient Egyptian for themselves (see middle section of each line):

ink As.t nTr.t
eenek Ah-set net-cher-et
I am Isis the goddess,

nb(.t) HkA
nebet hekah
possessor (or *Mistress*) *of Magic*

ir HkA
eer heka
who performs magic

Ax Dd mnx mdw
ahkh jed menakh medu
effective of speech, excellent of words.

For the magician it is vital to understand that by reading aloud the ancient Egyptian texts - especially if one can get their hands on a transliteration to create an approximate pronunciation – they will bring the hieroglyphs to life and their meanings into manifestation. Magical gestures could be employed for the active part of the spell. One such gesture is pointing the forefinger with the thumb pressed on top; this appears to have been used in spells to protect livestock during risky episodes, such as birth (Pinch, 2003). Other spells would involve writing on parchment and swallowing it; or pressing pins into clay images (Pinch, 2003). Such spells were particularly common during the Graeco-Roman period.

Tools of the Trade

A whole variety of different items and ingredients could be

used in Egyptian spells, depending on their availability for the magician. Priest-magicians and doctor-magicians would have had greater access to premium items and all doctors would have used magic alongside their medicinal prescriptions and operations (Pinch, 2003). Common people performing magic would have to make use of what was around them. Buried in a Middle Kingdom tomb, later covered by the mortuary temple of Ramesses II, was a magician's box. This box contained an assortment of magical implements, such as a superb serpent-shaped wand made of bronze, a masked figurine wielding two such wands, magic 'knives' and various other zoomorphic figurines (Maarten, 2012).

These are examples of magical tools available to a priest-magician. More humble items may include simple things, such as faience amulets, scraps of parchment to be swallowed and various organic materials. The modern magician could attempt to recreate exquisite tools, but more likely will look about the house with a creative license. One easy 'tool' would be using colour associations. Many magical traditions associate magical meanings to colours and the ancient Egyptian tradition was no different, except that the Egyptians had fewer words for various shades than we do in English today. Ancient Egyptian tended to have one word for warm colours, *desher* (i.e. red, orange and yellow), and one colour for cold colours, *wadj* (i.e. green and blue; Pinch, 2003). Generally speaking, the following associations were held:

Red/Orange/Yellow = Solar powers, protection and binding. Red was also associated with chaos.
Green & Black = Growth and regeneration.
Blue = Heavenly beings and divinity.

The ambiguity in some of these associations means that again the practitioner today must look at their surroundings and build their own connections. Arguably there is nothing inauthentic about contemporary innovation, for the Egyptians would have been creating things for their own context, just as we are today.

Symbols

The symbol and hieroglyph, *tyet,* was also called the 'Knot of Isis'. It is an amulet in the shape of a looped knot (not dissimilar to an Ankh-shape) which appears throughout ancient Egyptian history (Allen, 2014).

Tyet **Knot (Metropolitan Museum of Art, 00.4.39)**

The *tyet* appears on amulets buried with the dead as early as the 1st Dynasty (Griffiths, 1980). In one spell the *tyet* is evidently used during a funerary rite:

> *"Thou hast thy blood, Isis; thou hast thy power, Isis; (thou hast thy magic, Isis).*
>
> *Amulets are the magical protection of this Eldest One, restraining whoever would do him harm.*
>
> *This spell is to be said over a tie-amulet of red jasper anointed*

with the sap of the 'nX-imy-plant, strung on sycamore bast, and put at the throat of this blessed one (on the day of joining the earth)."
(*BD* 156)

The spell itself continues by stating it has been proven to work "a million times" and that it must be kept secret from all but the followers of Osiris-Unnofer. It is unclear what the placement at the throat means, but the text suggests that the knot was linked somehow to Isis and blood. It has been interpreted by some to represent a knot of fabric worn by menstruating women (Griffiths, J. 2001). Knots were popularly worn by women as a fashion piece around the waist during the Late Period onwards. Many sculptures spread through the classical world depicting Isis wearing the knot at her hips and breast (Bianchi, 1980). Because of these associations, the *tyet* could be used today as a symbol promoting women's health, or in matters concerning blood, literally and metaphorically.

The *ankh* hieroglyph, meaning 'life', was important to all deities in Egypt. Kings and Priests were shown holding the symbol towards the nose of Goddesses and Gods, offerings them the breath of life. The gift of the breath of life is central to Isis' mythology, and therefore the *ankh* can be interpreted as a symbol of Isis' life-giving power.

Isis' sacred animals also function as her personal symbols. This includes any birds, especially kites and falcons, as well as serpents and cows. Her bovine image can be recalled by the horned sun disk she wears atop her head and serves as a reminder of the magical powers she obtained through tricking the sun god. The serpent at her brow reminds us of her protective and defensive nature. The throne hieroglyph symbolises her sovereignty over all things. The writing of her name in hieroglyphs, including the throne, acts as a manifestation of the Goddess herself, especially when her name is read aloud.

Selected Prayers & Hymns

Most spells dedicated to Isis deal with matters pertaining to poisonous animal bites. Others deal with funerary rituals and rebirth into the afterlife. Provided here are a selection of prayers and hymns appealing to Isis for more general purposes.

Release me from all things bad

"O Isis, Great of Magic, Heal Me, Release me from all things bad and evil."

(*Papyrus Ebers* 2; Lesko, 1999, p.170)

I come and bring Isis an offering

"I come and bring Aset an offering,
for all life and strength are from Her.
I shake sistra to Her beautiful face
forever and ever."

(Siuda, 2009, p.62)

Hail Queen Isis!

"Hail Queen Isis! Mistress of Heaven, Star of the Sea, Great of Magic!
The inundation floods between your thighs,
All creatures are born of your womb.
Hail Queen Isis! Ardent lover and screeching kite of despair!
You enfold us in your wings,
And know all our pains and fears.
Hail Queen Isis! Nebet-Pet, Isis-Pelagia, Weret-Hekau!
Mother of the Sun and crescent-crowned bringer of tides,
May you rise eternal and always be with us…"

(Author's own prayer)

Hymn to Isis at Philae

Beside each line I have provided an approximated pronunciation guide of the transliterated hieroglyphs in parentheses (capitalised letters are emphasised sounds):

(Chorus:) *"Praise to you Isis-Hathor,* (ee-Ah-oo net Aset Hut-Hor)
God's Mother, Lady of Heaven, (moot netcher nebet pet)
Mistress of Abaton, queen of the gods. (Henut ee-Aht wabet eeteet netcheru)

You are the divine mother of Horus, (netet moot netcher en Her)
The Mighty Bull, avenger of his father, (ka neKhet nedj-tee en eet-ef)
Who causes the rebels to fall. (dee-ef seKher seb-ee-oo)

(Chorus)

You are the divine mother of Horus, (netet moot netcher en Her)
Min-Horus, the hero who smites his enemy, (menoo-Hor per-ah Hoo Khefety-ef)
And makes a massacre thereby. (eer nes en-eem)

(Chorus)

You are the divine mother of Horus, (netet moot netcher en Her)
Khonsu-the-powerful, the royal child of the Lord of Eternity, (Khonsu neKhet neKhen nesoo en neb djet)
Lord of Nubia, ruler of the foreign lands. (neb tAh setee HekA KhA-soot)

(Chorus)

You are the divine mother of Horus, (netet moot netcher en Her)
The Mighty Bull, who establishes the temples of the Ennead, (kA neKhet semen gesu-peru pes-djet)
nd fashions every divine image. (eer nen neb)

(Chorus)

You are the divine mother of Horus, (netet moot netcher en Her)
The Mighty Bull who protects Egypt, (kA neKhet Khoo bAket)
Lord of the Nome, for ever. (neb spat djet)

(Chorus)
(Inscription from the Temple of Philae; Žabkar, 1983, p. 118)

Praising Isis at Philae

"O Isis, the Great, God's Mother, Lady of Philae,
God's Wife, God's Adorer, and God's Hand,
God's Mother and Great Royal Spouse,
Adornment and lady of the Ornaments of the Palace.
Lady and desire of the green fields,
Nursling who fills the palace with her beauty,
Fragrance of the palace, mistress of joy,
Who runs her course in the Divine Place.
Rain-cloud which makes green (the fields) when it descends,
Maiden, sweet of Love, Lady of Upper and Lower Egypt,
Who issues orders among the divine Ennead,
According to whose command one rules.
Princess, great of praise, lady of charm,
Whose face loves the joy of fresh myrrh."
(Inscription from the Temple of Philae; Žabkar, 1983, pp. 129-130)

A Contemporary Pagan Perspective

Pagans today typically take inspiration from the past and bring it forward to the modern day. For some, access to written primary sources are scarce or have been manipulated by Christian authors. Such may be the case for those taking inspiration from the Celtic or Norse traditions. We are fortunate that a great deal of religious and magical information survives from ancient Egypt (even though an awful lot has been lost). With this material one can easily piece together rituals and spells and recite ancient prayers. To the ancient Egyptians there appears to have been distinctive differences between the religious practices of priests within temples and those of the common people. Indeed, there wasn't one Egyptian religion, but many! Pagans today often mix the Egyptian myths, practices and traditions according to their needs and preferences. Based on the surviving sources we may create our own Egyptian-style spells, rituals and prayers so long as we retain the basic principles and structure:

1. To depict something, and/or to speak written words aloud made them real.
2. Similar or associated things can be used to affect other similar things (sympathetic magic).
3. To speak the true name of something gave you power over it.
4. Spells are created with two main parts: 1) Words to be said and 2) things to be done.

The priesthood would have, for the most part, remained loyal to their archaic rituals, placing value in what was already ancient to them. The common people may have continued their own practices as handed down through the family; however, lacking any formal texts (or the ability to read) meant that domestic religion would have had more potential for changes. Innovation and flexibility are always an option for non-dogmatic religion.

Conclusions

Worshipping Isis Today

Recreating Rituals

We are greatly fortunate that so much material from the ancient cult of Isis survives to this day. From the material gathered in the preceding chapters it is easily possible to reconstruct and innovate ancient practices of the Isian cult today. From historical records and archaeology, we have the raw materials needed to recreate rituals and to fill in the gaps with new material relevant to us in a modern context. An example of this would be for those living by the seaside or even a large lake, who want to observe the *navigium Isidis*. On the 5th March a group of like-minded individuals may lead a procession to the water's edge, adorned with floral garlands and dressed in white clothing. Whilst we do not know the exact songs sung to Isis, there are many prayers and hymns that can be adapted, as well as new compositions! The procession could make their way shaking sistra – or any available percussion instruments – and offer milk, bread, beer, and flowers to the water. Paper boats could be released upon the waves to signify those who travel upon the sea. The purpose of the festival could be the same today as it was in the past: giving thanks to the sea and the life-giving waters, asking Isis to keep our seafarers safe and praying that she brings abundance to our shores. It matters not that we know little else of the festival activities, as we have the central essence to build upon.

The same can be said for the rituals pertaining to the initiated Isiasci. Thanks to Apuleius, we have an outline to follow if we so choose. The descriptions of initiation above may sound familiar to Pagan ears today. Many magical traditions contain an initiatory element, often requiring a symbolic death and rebirth to occur (Farrar & Farrar, 1984). Mystery traditions provide opportunities for initiates to have direct personal experiences with the divine, without intermediaries (Bowden, 2010) and this is an attractive aspect of many contemporary and neo-Pagan traditions today.

Creating a Shrine and/or Altar

Shrines and altars are completely unique to every individual. A shrine is a sacred space allocated to the veneration of an entity, be that ancestor, spirit or deity. An altar may also be a space for veneration; however, an altar additionally functions as a space for conducting rituals and magic. As a devotee of Isis, this may indeed form a part of your spiritual practice. A shrine or altar dedicated to Isis can be as simple or elaborate as you like. It will usually include some form of light, perhaps from a candle or a lantern. If possible, you could include a safe container for incense, as well as an offering bowl to offer the Goddess milk, beer, bread, honey, flowers, and clean water. You may choose to add other things such as her symbols, feathers, special stones, figurines or art. In whatever way you decide to adorn your altar, it will only have power if it means something to you. What do you associate with Isis? What reminds you of her? Do you identify more with Aset than Isis, the other way around, or both together? Your altar may be bedecked in luscious fabrics and shining statuettes; or it may be a candle and a home-made clay bowl. Either way, Isis hears your prayers, both spoken and silent. By creating an intentional space to honour her you have accepted the invitation for divine dialogue.

A key part of contemporary Paganism is our ability to reconstruct and innovate ancient religious practices. We can access aspects of ancient practices thanks to the efforts of professional researchers. We are then able to use this knowledge to reconstruct and innovate ancient ideas, creating new forms. By doing so, we fill in the gaps in knowledge and address contemporary needs. As emphasised throughout this work,

Isis is a Goddess who has always called to a variety of different people across time and cultures. Likewise, her worship can be expressed in a diverse array of ways and undergo constant changes. It always has done.

* * *

It is hopefully clear from this book that Isis is a diverse Goddess, whose wings stretch across time and geography. Her mythic narrative takes her from playing the trickster, the wife and queen to become a grieving widow, mother, and a healer. She has dominion over the magical and healing arts, over the sun and moon, the stars, earth, rivers, harvests, and seas. Her name has been sung for 4500 years, across North Africa, the near East, the Mediterranean and into Europe and Britain. For a time, her sacred significance was been downplayed due to the arrival of new religious ideas; however, over the last century her worship has seen a remarkable revival. Dion Fortune's famous novel, 'The Sea Priestess' (originally published in 1938), features Isis as the divine teacher of a contemporary Priestess; this work has been influential to many within the Goddess revival.

Organisations such as the Fellowship of Isis are "dedicated to honouring the Goddess in her many forms", using Isis as the figurehead for the universality of the Divine Feminine (Fellowship of Isis website). Temples are being erected in her name, such as the aforementioned Isis Oasis, and revival groups such as Kemetic Orthodox are worshipping her Egyptian form as Aset (kemet.org). For myself, when someone says the name 'Isis,' my heart and mind automatically translate 'Goddess'; Isis *is* the embodiment of the Divine Feminine to me. Such a concept may be difficult for contemporary hard polytheists to accept, and that is fine; however, it would have been perfectly acceptable for the ancient Egyptians to name Isis as the Great Mother of all the Gods, and then to say the same about Hathor, or Mut moments after. Isis is the ultimate shapeshifting Goddess and this, combined with her empathy for the human condition, is why she has survived to this day. In my view, many Pagan deities change shape in order to communicate most effectively with as many different individuals as possible. Everyone has different expectations, needs and perspectives and I believe Divinity reaches us each in a unique way (explaining the multitudes of religions out there). Whether one sees her in her traditional form as the solar-magician Goddess Aset, or in her lunar maternal form as Isis, she is a shapeshifting Goddess with extraordinary magical ability. Isis is a Goddess who is a mother to all people. Isis does not discriminate against one person or the next. It matters not where you are from, your gender, sexuality, class or profession. Isis is a timeless Goddess who is just as relevant to a 21st century westerner living in a British sea-side town, as she was to the infamous Queen Cleopatra VII over two thousand years ago.

Ultimately, whatever aspect of Isis you identify with most, Isis is a Goddess sympathetic to the human experience, who understands our deepest feelings. If you open your heart to her, she will open her wings to you. And if you happen to be looking for an ally in your magical workings, there is none better than she!

Bibliography

Primary Sources

Allen, J. (2015) *The ancient Egyptian pyramid texts [translated] by James P. Allen,* Atlanta, SBL Press.

Apuleius, *Metamorphoses.* trans. S. Ruden (2011) New Haven, Yale University Press.

British Museum online catalogue, items EA36250 and EA52831. Available at https://research.britishmuseum.org/research/collection_online/search.aspx. (Accessed 19 April 2019).

Kelly Simpson, W. (2003) *'The Contendings of Horus and Seth'* (translated by M. Broze), in (ed Kelly Simpson, W.) *The Literature of Ancient Egypt: An Anthology of Stories, Instructions, Stelae, Autobiographies, and Poetry* (third edition), London, Yale University Press, pp. 91-103.

Calverley, A., Broome, M., Gardiner, A. (1933) *The Temple of King Sethos I at Abydos. Volume1: The Chapels of Osiris, Isis and Horus,* London, The Egypt Exploration Society.

Faulkner, R. (1936) 'The Bremner-Rhind Papyrus: I. A. The Songs of Isis and Nephthys', *The Journal of Egyptian Archaeology,* vol. 22, no. 2, pp. 121-140.

Faulkner, R. (2007) *The Ancient Egyptian Coffin Texts,* Oxford, Aris et Phillips.

Herodotus, *The Histories, vol. 2.* trans. A. Godley (1975), Massachusetts, Harvard University Press.

Hesiod, *Theogony.* trans. R. Lattimore (1991), Ann Arbor, The University of Michigan Press.

Homeric Hymn to Demeter. trans. M. West (2003), London, Harvard University Press.

J. Paul Getty Museum Collection online, item 71.AB.180. Available at: http://www.getty.edu/art/collection/ (Accessed 25 January 2020).

Kelly Simpson, W. et al. (2003) 'Book of the Dead 125: "The Negative Confession"', in (ed Kelly Simpson, W.) *The Literature of Ancient Egypt: An Anthology of Stories, Instructions, Stelae, Autobiographies, and Poetry* (third edition), London, Yale University Press, pp. 267-277.

Lichtheim, M. (1973) *Ancient Egyptian Literature* (vol. 1), Berkeley, University of California Press.

Lichtheim, M. (1976) *Ancient Egyptian Literature* (vol. 2), Berkeley, University of California Press.

Metropolitan Museum of Art collection online, item 00.4.39. Available at: https://www.metmuseum.org/art/collection (Accessed 25 January 2020).

Museo Archaeologico Nazionale di Napoli website, 'Temple of Isis Exhibition'. Available at: https://www.museoarcheologiconapoli.it/en/room-and-sections-of-the-exhibition/temple-of-isis/ (Accessed 5 January 2020).

Museum of London online collection, item 77.57. Available at: https://collections.museumoflondon.org.uk/online/ (Accessed 12 January 2020).

Nederhof, M. J. (2008) *Papyrus Westcar* [Online]. Available at: https://rhbarnhart.net/westcar-nederhof.pdf. (Accessed 4 January 2020).

Plutarch, *Moralia, Vol. 5, 'Isis and Osiris'*. trans. F. C. Babbitt (1936) London, Harvard University Press.

Žabkar, L. (1983) 'Six Hymns to Isis in the Sanctuary of Her Temple at Philae and Their Theological Significance. Part I', *The Journal of Egyptian Archaeology*, vol. 69, pp. 115-137.

Secondary Sources

Allen, J. (2014) *Middle Egyptian: An Introduction to the Language and Culture of Hieroglyphs*, Cambridge: Cambridge University Press.

Al Shafei, H. K. (2016) 'The Crowns of Cleopatra VII: An Iconographical Analytical Study', *Journal of Applied Sciences in Cultural Heritage*, vol. 2, no. 2, pp. 29-38 [Online]. Available at:

http://www.sci-cult.com/files (Accessed 26 January 2020).

Assmann, J. (2005). *Death and salvation in ancient Egypt* (trans. D. Lorton), Ithaca, Cornell University Press.

Assmann, J. (2008) 'Translating Gods: Religion as a Factor of Cultural (Un)Translatability', in (ed H. de Vries) *Religion: Beyond a Concept,* Fordham University Press.

Bailleul-LeSuer, R. (2012) 'Birds in Creation Myths', in (ed Bailleul-LeSuer, R.) *Between Heaven and Earth. Birds in Ancient Egypt,* Chicago, Oriental Institute Museum Publications, pp. 131-134.

Barthell, E. (1971). *Gods and goddesses of ancient Greece,* Coral Gables: University of Miami Press.

Bianchi, R. (1980) 'Knot the Isis-Knot', *Bulletin of the Egyptological Seminar of New York,* vol. 2, pp. 9-31.

Blackman, A.M & Fairman, H.W. (1942) 'The Myth of Horus at Edfu: II. C. The Triumph of Horus over His Enemies: A Sacred Drama', *Journal of Egyptian Archaeology,* vol. 28, pp. 32-38.

Bowden, H. (2010) *Mystery Cults in the Ancient World,* London, Thames & Hudson.

Breasted, J. (2010) *Development of Religion and Thought in Ancient Egypt,* New York, Cosimo Classics.

Brewer, D. and Teeter, E. (2007) *Egypt and the Egyptians,* Cambridge, Cambridge University Press.

Buhl, M. (1947) 'The Goddesses of the Egyptian Tree Cult,' *Journal of Near Eastern Studies,* vol. 6, no. 2, pp. 80-97.

Clauss, M. (2000). *The Roman cult of Mithras: The god and his mysteries* (trans. R. Gordon), Edinburgh, Edinburgh University Press.

Constanza Centrone, M. (2004) *Egyptian Corn Mummies,* unpublished PhD thesis, Swansea, University of Wales Swansea.

Craig Patch, D. (2011) 'Introduction' *Dawn of Egyptian Art* (ed Craig Patch, D.), Yale University Press, New Haven, pp. 3-20.

Delia, D. (1998) 'Isis, or the Moon,' in *Egyptian Religion. The Last Thousand Years. Studies Dedicated to the Memory of Jan Quaege-*

beur (eds Clarysse, W., Schoors, A. and Willems, H.), Leuven, Peeters Publishers, vol. 1, pp. 539-550.

Daumas, F. (1958) *Les Mammisis des temples égyptiens,* Paris, Les Belles Lettres.

Donalson, M. D. (2003) *The Cult of Isis in the Roman Empire: Isis Invicta,* New York, E. Mellen Press.

Farrar, J. and Farrar, S. (1984) *A Witches' Bible. The Complete Witches' Handbook,* London, Robert Hale Publications.

Faulkner, R. (1962) *A Concise Dictionary of Middle Egyptian,* Oxford, Griffith Institute.

Fellowship of Isis website. Available at: http://www.fellowshipofisis.com/ (Accessed 23 July 2018).

Fortune, D. (1938) *The Sea Priestess,* San Francisco: Red Wheel (2003).

Gilula, M. (1971) 'Coffin Texts Spell 148', *The Journal of Egyptian Archaeology,* vol. 57, pp. 14-19. Available at: doi:10.2307/3855939 (Accessed 12 July 2018).

Green, M. (1983) 'Isis at Thornborough,' *Records of Buckinghamshire,* vol. 25, pp. 139-141.

Griffiths, J. G. (1980) *The Origins of Osiris and His Cult,* Leiden, E.J. Brill.

Griffiths, J. G. (2001) "Isis", in (ed D. Redford) *The Oxford Encyclopedia of Ancient Egypt*, Oxford, Oxford University Press, pp. 188-191.

Hackworth Peterson, L. (2016) 'The Places of Roman Isis: Between Egyptomania, Politics, and Religion', *Classical Studies, Egyptology, Classical Religions and Mythologies* [Online]. Available at: https://www.oxfordhandbooks.com/search (Accessed 7 December 2019).

Hart, G. (2005) *The Routledge dictionary of Egyptian gods and goddesses* (second edition), London, Routledge.

Higgins, S. (2012) 'Divine Mothers: The Influence of Isis on the Virgin Mary in Egyptian Lactans-Iconography' *Journal of the Canadian Society for Coptic Studies*, vol.3, no.4, pp. 71-90.

Hornung, E. (1996) *Conceptions of God in ancient Egypt: The one and the many* (trans. J. Baines), Ithaca, Cornell University Press.

Ikram, S. (2003) *Death and Burial in Ancient Egypt*, London, Pearson Education.

Isis Oasis Retreat Centre website. Available at: http://www.isisoasis.us/ (Accessed 27 January 2020).

Jones, P. J. (2017) 'Africa: Greek and Roman Perspectives from Homer to Apuleius', *Center for Hellenic Studies*, Harvard University [online]. Available at: https://chs.harvard.edu/CHS/article/display/6535.prudence-j-jones-africa-greek-and-roman-perspectives-from-homer-to-apuleius (Accessed 7 January 2020).

Kemetic Orthodox website. Available at: http://www.kemet.org (Accessed 4 September 2018).

Kockelmann, H. (2011) 'Birth House (Mammisi)', (ed. W. Wendrich), *UCLA Encyclopaedia of Egyptology*, pp. 1-7. Available at: http://digital2.library.ucla.edu/viewItem.do?ark=21198/zz0026wfgr (Accessed 12 December 2019).

Lesko, B. (1999) *The Great Goddesses of Egypt,* Norman, University of Oklahoma Press.

Lloyd, A. B. (2003) 'The Ptolemaic Period (332-30 BC)', in (ed I. Shaw) *The Oxford history of ancient Egypt edited by Ian Shaw.* Oxford, Oxford University Press, pp. 188-413.

Maarten, R. (2012) *Egyptian Magic. The Quest for Thoth's Book of Secrets,* Cairo, The American University in Cairo Press.

Malek, J. (2003) 'The Old Kingdom', (ed I. Shaw) *The Oxford History of Ancient Egypt,* Oxford, Oxford University Press, pp. 83-107.

McCabe, E. (2008) *An examination of the Isis Cult with Preliminary Exploration into New Testament Studies*, Maryland, University Press of America.

Meeks, D. and Favard-Meeks, C., (1999) *Daily life of the Egyptian gods*, London, Pimlico.

Merrifield, R. (1983) *London, City of the Romans*, London, Batsford

Ltd.

Peacock, D. (2003) 'The Roman Period', in (ed I. Shaw) *The Oxford history of ancient Egypt,* Oxford, Oxford University Press, pp. 414-436.

Pinch, G. (2002) *Egyptian Mythology. A guide to the Gods, Goddesses and Traditions of Ancient Egypt,* Oxford, Oxford University Press.

Ruether, R. & Radford, R. (2005) *Goddesses and the Divine Feminine: A Western Religious History,* Berkeley, University of California Press. Pinch, G. (2006) *Magic in Ancient Egypt,* London, British Museum Press.

Ritner, R. (2008) *The Mechanics of Ancient Egyptian Magical Practice*, Chicago, The Oriental Institute of the University of Chicago.

Roberts, A. (1995) *Hathor Rising: The Serpent Power of Ancient Egypt,* Rottingdean, Northgate Publishers.

Roberts, A. (2000) *My Heart My Mother: Death and Rebirth in Ancient Egypt,* Rottingdean, Northgate Publishers.

Salem, M. S. (1937) 'The *Lychnapsia Philocaliana* and the Birthday of Isis', *Journal of Roman Studies,* vol. 27, pp. 165-167.

Scheid, J. (2003) *An Introduction to Roman Religion* (trans. J. Lloyd) Edinburgh, Edinburgh University Press.

Scott, N. (1951) 'The Metternich Stela', *The Metropolitan Museum of Art Bulletin,* vol. 9, no. 8, pp. 201-217.

Shaw, I. (2003) *The Oxford history of ancient Egypt edited by Ian Shaw,* Oxford, Oxford University Press.

Siuda, T. (2009) *The Ancient Egyptian Prayerbook,* Portland, Stargazer Design.

Smith, M. (2010) *God is Translation: Deities in Cross-cultural Discourse in the Biblical World,* Cambridge, Wm. B. Eerdmans Publishing.

Stadler, M. A. (2017) 'New Light on the Universality of Isis', in (eds S. Nagel, J. F. Quack and C. Witschel) *Entangled Worlds: Religious Confluences between East and West in the Roman Em-*

pire. The Cults of Isis, Mithras and Jupiter Dolichenus, Tübingen, Mohr Siebeck, pp. 232–243.

Stevenson, S., Smith, C. and Madden, F. (1889) *A Dictionary of Roman Coins, REpublicaiton and Imperial*, London, G. Bell and Sons.

Swetnam-Burland, M. (2002) Egypt in the Roman Imagination: A Study of Aegyptiaca from Pompeii, PhD thesis, Ann Arbor, University of Michigan. Available at: https://search.proquest.com/docview/305535572 (Accessed 11 November 2019).

Swetnam-Burland, M. (2015) *Egypt in Italy: Visions of Egypt in Roman Imperial Culture*, New York, Cambridge University Press.

Takács, S. (2008) 'Initiations and Mysteries in Apuleius' Metamorphoses', *Ancient Mysteries: Modern Secrets a Special Themed Issue of Electronic Antiquity*, vol. 12, no. 1, pp. 73-87 [Online]. Available at: https://scholar.lib.vt.edu/ejournals/ElAnt/V12 N1/takacs.pdf (Accessed 1 December 2019).

Teeter, E. (2011) *Religion and Ritual in Ancient Egypt*, Cambridge, Cambridge University Press.

Tower Hollis, S. (2009) 'Hathor and Isis in Byblos in the Second and First Millennia BCE', *Journal of Ancient Egyptian Interconnections*, vol. 1, no. 2, pp. 1-8.

Tyldesley, J. (2006) *Chronicle of the Queens of Egypt. From Early Dynastic Times to the Death of Cleopatra*, London, Thames & Hudson.

UNESCO website, 'Philae (Egypt)'. Available at: https://en.unesco.org/ (Accessed 5 January 2020).

Valdesogo, M. R. (2020) 'A Challenge in the Art of Ancient Egypt: Osirian Solar Iconography', *María Rosa Valdesogo*, 19 January 2015. Available at: http://www.mariarosavaldesogo.com/challenge-art-ancient-egypt-osirian-solar-iconography/ (Accessed: 27 January 2020)

Verner, M. (2012) *Temple of the World: Sanctuaries, Cults, and Mysteries of Ancient Egypt* (trans. A. Bryson-Gustová), Cairo, The American University in Cairo.

Walters, J. (1995) 'Egyptian Religion in Ephesos', in (ed H. Koester) *Ephesos. Metropolis of Asia: An Interdisciplinary Approach to its Archaeology, Religion, and Culture*, Trinity Press International, pp. 281-310.

Wilkinson, R. (2000) *The Complete Temples of Ancient Egypt*, London, Thames & Hudson.

Wilkinson, R. (2003) *The Complete Gods and Goddesses of Ancient Egypt*, London, Thames & Hudson.

**MOON
BOOKS**

PAGANISM & SHAMANISM

What is Paganism? A religion, a spirituality, an alternative belief system, nature worship? You can find support for all these definitions (and many more) in dictionaries, encyclopaedias, and text books of religion, but subscribe to any one and the truth will evade you. Above all Paganism is a creative pursuit, an encounter with reality, an exploration of meaning and an expression of the soul. Druids, Heathens, Wiccans and others, all contribute their insights and literary riches to the Pagan tradition. Moon Books invites you to begin or to deepen your own encounter, right here, right now. If you have enjoyed this book, why not tell other readers by posting a review on your preferred book site.

Recent bestsellers from Moon Books are:

Journey to the Dark Goddess
How to Return to Your Soul
Jane Meredith
Discover the powerful secrets of the Dark Goddess and
transform your depression, grief and pain into healing
and integration.
Paperback: 978-1-84694-677-6 ebook: 978-1-78099-223-5

Shamanic Reiki
Expanded Ways of Working with Universal Life Force Energy
Llyn Roberts, Robert Levy
Shamanism and Reiki are each powerful ways of healing; together,
their power multiplies. *Shamanic Reiki* introduces techniques to
help healers and Reiki practitioners tap ancient healing wisdom.
Paperback: 978-1-84694-037-8 ebook: 978-1-84694-650-9

Pagan Portals – The Awen Alone
Walking the Path of the Solitary Druid
Joanna van der Hoeven
An introductory guide for the solitary Druid, *The Awen Alone* will
accompany you as you explore, and seek out your own place
within the natural world.
Paperback: 978-1-78279-547-6 ebook: 978-1-78279-546-9

A Kitchen Witch's World of Magical Herbs & Plants
Rachel Patterson
A journey into the magical world of herbs and plants, filled with
magical uses, folklore, history and practical magic. By popular
writer, blogger and kitchen witch, Tansy Firedragon.
Paperback: 978-1-78279-621-3 ebook: 978-1-78279-620-6

Medicine for the Soul
The Complete Book of Shamanic Healing
Ross Heaven
All you will ever need to know about shamanic healing and how to
become your own shaman...
Paperback: 978-1-78099-419-2 ebook: 978-1-78099-420-8

Shaman Pathways – The Druid Shaman
Exploring the Celtic Otherworld
Danu Forest
A practical guide to Celtic shamanism with exercises and
techniques as well as traditional lore for exploring the Celtic
Otherworld.
Paperback: 978-1-78099-615-8 ebook: 978-1-78099-616-5

Traditional Witchcraft for the Woods and Forests
A Witch's Guide to the Woodland with Guided Meditations and
Pathworking
Mélusine Draco
A Witch's guide to walking alone in the woods, with guided
meditations and pathworking.
Paperback: 978-1-84694-803-9 ebook: 978-1-84694-804-6

Naming the Goddess
Trevor Greenfield
Naming the Goddess is written by over eighty adherents and
scholars of Goddess and Goddess Spirituality.
Paperback: 978-1-78279-476-9 ebook: 978-1-78279-475-2

Shapeshifting into Higher Consciousness
Heal and Transform Yourself and Our World with Ancient
Shamanic and Modern Methods
Llyn Roberts
Ancient and modern methods that you can use every day to
transform yourself and make a positive difference in the world.
Paperback: 978-1-84694-843-5 ebook: 978-1-84694-844-2

Readers of ebooks can buy or view any of these bestsellers by
clicking on the live link in the title. Most titles are published in
paperback and as an ebook. Paperbacks are available in traditional
bookshops. Both print and ebook formats are available online.

Find more titles and sign up to our readers' newsletter at
http://www.johnhuntpublishing.com/paganism
Follow us on Facebook at https://www.facebook.com/MoonBooks
and Twitter at https://twitter.com/MoonBooksJHP